Megaregional China

This book unravels China's new megaregional structure, new megaregional planning and development, new megaregional governance, and new regional planning system. It draws upon a diversity of megaregional cases: city clusters of the Beijing–Tianjin–Hebei region, Yangtze River delta region, and Greater Bay Area; and metropolitan circles of Chengdu, Hangzhou, Hong Kong, Shanghai, Shenzhen, and Zhengzhou.

Megaregions are the new form of Chinese-style urbanisation. China's new discourse of 'high-quality development' and 'new-type urbanisation' is reshaping its megaregional strategy. Imbalance and fragmentation characterise the diversity of megaregions—developed or developing, coastal or inland. The central goal of megaregional planning and governance is to achieve integrated, balanced development of them. Hu challenges the official notion of 'top-level design' that dominates the planning, governance, and development of China's megaregions. Instead, he argues for the importance of engaging nongovernmental stakeholders, rebalancing the government-market relationality, encouraging bottom-up initiatives, and enabling grassroots ingenuity.

The volume offers the first and most comprehensive study of megaregional China in the new contexts of both national development and urban development. It will be of interest to anyone looking into urban and regional development, and Chinese studies.

Richard Hu is an award-winning urban planner. His work and interests—both intellectual and professional—integrate built environment, economy, and technology to address contemporary urban transformation and sustainable development, with a focus on the Asia-Pacific region. He is the author of *Smart Design* (2021) and *The Shenzhen Phenomenon* (2020).

Routledge Research in Sustainable Planning and Development in Asia
Series Editor: **Richard Hu**

Urban Flood Risk Management
Looking at Jakarta
Christopher Silver

Data-centric Regenerative Built Environment
Big Data for Sustainable Regeneration
Saeed Banihashemi and Sepideh Zarepour Sohi

Disaster Resilience and Sustainability
Japan's Urban Development and Social Capital
Hitomi Nakanishi

Megaregional China
Richard Hu

For more information about this series, please visit: www.routledge.com/Routledge-Research-in-Sustainable-Planning-and-Development-in-Asia/book-series/RRSPDA

Megaregional China

Richard Hu

LONDON AND NEW YORK

First published 2024
by Routledge
4 Park Square, Milton Park, Abingdon, Oxon OX14 4RN

and by Routledge
605 Third Avenue, New York, NY 10158

Routledge is an imprint of the Taylor & Francis Group, an informa business

© 2024 Richard Hu

The right of Richard Hu to be identified as author of this work has been asserted in accordance with sections 77 and 78 of the Copyright, Designs and Patents Act 1988.

All rights reserved. No part of this book may be reprinted or reproduced or utilised in any form or by any electronic, mechanical, or other means, now known or hereafter invented, including photocopying and recording, or in any information storage or retrieval system, without permission in writing from the publishers.

Trademark notice: Product or corporate names may be trademarks or registered trademarks, and are used only for identification and explanation without intent to infringe.

British Library Cataloguing in Publication Data
A catalogue record for this book is available from the British Library

ISBN: 978-0-367-62199-5 (hbk)
ISBN: 978-0-367-62220-6 (pbk)
ISBN: 978-1-003-10840-5 (ebk)

DOI: 10.4324/9781003108405

Typeset in Times New Roman
by KnowledgeWorks Global Ltd.

Contents

List of figures vi
List of tables vii
Acknowledgements viii
List of abbreviations ix

1 Megaregions and urban China 1

2 Planning megaregions 16

3 Developing metropolitan circles: Issues and challenges 35

4 The dragon's head in spatial imaginary: Integrating Shanghai and the Yangtze River delta region 58

5 'One country, two cities': Relational planning of Shenzhen and Hong Kong in the Greater Bay Area 76

Index 94

Figures

1.1	Urbanisation rate and GDP per capita: China versus the world, 1978–2022	3
1.2	Spatial structure of megaregional China	7
2.1	Regional plan in the new Chinese planning system	19
2.2	Beijing–Tianjin–Hebei region	24
2.3	Spatial structure for development of the Chengdu metropolitan circle	31
3.1	Annual GDP growth rates: China versus the world, 1978–2022	36
3.2	Hangzhou's economic base in the Chinese economy, 2010–2019	41
3.3	Vertical intergovernmental imbalance in financial powers and financial responsibilities	49
4.1	Yangtze River delta	60
4.2	Wanjiang urban belt	64
4.3	G60 Innovation Corridor	69
4.4	Greater Shanghai metropolitan circle	72
5.1	Greater Bay Area	78
5.2	Strategic concept plan for *Hong Kong 2030*	84
5.3	Conceptual spatial framework for *Hong Kong 2030+*	86
5.4	GDP of Shenzhen and Hong Kong, 1980–2020	89

Tables

2.1	Planning the trio of city clusters	21
3.1	Fiscal revenues and fiscal expenditures between the central government and local governments, 2019	50
3.2	Major investment projects in the Chengdu metropolitan circle, 2022	55
4.1	Major indicators for the three provinces and one municipality in the Yangtze River delta region, 2020	61
4.2	GDP of major cities in the Wanjiang urban belt (in RMB 100 million), 2009–2021	65

Acknowledgements

This little book is integral to my research of China's urbanisation and transformation. But its focus on megaregional China is related to my involvement with a collaborative project between the World Bank and the China Center for Urban Development in 2021–2022. This collaborative project concerned metropolitan regional governance in China. It triggered my interest in further studying China's megaregional planning and governance, which in turn has led to the fruition of this book. Chapter 3 of this book is largely built upon my work for this collaborative project. I acknowledge the contributions in various forms from other participants of the project, but I am responsible for the content.

This book has a dialogue with my book *Reinventing the Chinese City* (2023) through building upon the latter's focus on China's urbanisation and extending it in the new direction of megaregionalisation. Several key concepts and practices for China's new urbanisation strategy are recapped and examined at length here in regard to their relevance to megaregions.

Chapter 5 of this book draws upon certain material and ideas about the relationality between Shenzhen and Hong Kong in my book *The Shenzhen Phenomenon* (2020). But they are significantly adapted and updated here to reflect the new situation that has been unfolding since that book's publication.

Abbreviations

CEPA	Closer Economic Partnership Arrangement
CMCOCDO	Chengdu Metropolitan Circle One-City Development Office
CPC	Communist Party of China
DAM	direct-administered municipality
FDI	foreign direct investment
GDP	gross domestic product
HKSARG	Hong Kong Special Administrative Region Government
HPDRC	Henan Provincial Development and Reform Commission
HSR	high-speed rail
LQ	location quotient
MHURD	Ministry for Housing and Urban-Rural Development
MNR	Ministry of Natural Resources
NDRC	National Development and Reform Commission
PLC	prefecture-level city
PPP	public-private partnership
PRC	People's Republic of China
PRD	Pearl River Delta
R&D	research and development
SAR	special administrative region
SEZ	special economic zone
SOE	state-owned enterprise
SHPNRB	Shanghai Planning and Natural Resources Bureau
SZPNRB	Shenzhen Planning and Natural Resources Bureau
TOD	Transit-oriented development

1 Megaregions and urban China

Mao Zedong's portrait is hung at Tiananmen, China's icon of centrality and power. His body is embalmed in his memorial hall, sitting in the middle of Tiananmen Square. These tell the status of Mao in China. Mao achieved this status for good reasons. Mao and his party, the Communist Party of China (CPC), established the People's Republic of China (PRC) in 1949. For over one century, since 1840 when China was first invaded by the British army during the Opium War, this ancient nation had suffered waves of foreign invasions and domestic chaos, conflicts, and wars. Generations of Chinese elites and revolutionaries had made efforts to reunify and rebuild a great nation. Only Mao and his party made it.

Over the two-millennium history of the Chinese empire, a group of emperors had unified the nation, established new regimes, and started new dynasties. In many senses, Mao was one of them. But Mao seemed to be the only one who changed China dramatically, not only during his time of rule but also after his death. In a way, the change to China after Mao's death was no less dramatic than when he was alive. Mao's rule of China was largely based on a combination of home-made feudalism (in the Chinese context) and imported communism, probably the most undesirable scenario for governing the transition of an ancient society to modernity. Mao's China was no better—even worse in certain aspects—than pre-Mao times; it was one of isolation, poverty, and lack of freedoms.

Mao Zedong died on 9 September 1976, still in his position as the paramount leader of China. Within one month, Mao's wife, Jiang Qing, and three other Maoist proponents—the so-called Gang of Four—were arrested. With Mao's death and the arrest of his followers, the decade-long Cultural Revolution (1966–1976) initiated and manipulated by Mao was terminated. Within several years, the successor selected by Mao, Hua Guofeng, was sidelined in the post-Mao power restructuring of the CPC. Deng Xiaoping became the new paramount leader through his experience, capability, authority, and cunning. Deng was a comrade of Mao and had been oppressed by Mao for following a 'capitalist' line. Mao's death cleared the way for Deng to pursue his line, which, for Deng, was never 'capitalist' but 'socialist'. In 1978,

DOI: 10.4324/9781003108405-1

Deng Xiaoping formally launched 'reform and opening-up', a modernisation agenda that fundamentally reversed the previous Maoist line.

An urban China—as we know it today—started in 1978.

Chinese-style urbanisation

Maoist China was a rural society, remaining almost static in urbanisation. In 1950, China's urbanisation rate—measured by the share of urban residents in the total population—was 11.8 per cent; in 1976 when Mao died, it was 17.5 per cent (United Nations, 2018). During Mao's time, China was a stringently dual urban-rural society in terms of access to rights, resources, and opportunities. This social divide still lingers on today, and its influences are profound and enduring: some are salient; some are latent.

To illustrate the drastic changes in post-1978 China, Figure 1.1 compares the urbanisation rate and gross domestic product (GDP) per capita—two correlated indicators—of China and the world from 1978 to 2020:

- In 1978: China's urbanisation rate was 17.9 per cent and the world's was 38.5 per cent; China's GDP per capita was US$156 and the world's average was US$2,026—nearly 13 times the former.
- In 2022: China's urbanisation rate was 63.6 per cent, and the world's was 56.9 per cent; its GDP per capita was a bit higher than the world's average—both were more than US$12,000.

In 2013, China's urbanisation rate surpassed the world's; in 2021, China's GDP per capita surpassed the world's average. In around four decades, China has been marching rapidly into a highly urbanised society. It is also getting close to the World Bank's benchmark line of high-income countries: gross national income (GNI) per capita of more than current US$13,845 as of 1 July 2023 (Hamadeh et al., 2023).

Post-1978 China is still an ongoing and evolving story; this story is frequently retold in new contexts, however. In the recent decade, several macro transformations have been emerging and are likely to reshape the country's future development, including its urban development, until the mid of the 21st century. These macro transformations include, among other things, transformative urbanisation, a new principal contradiction identified for national development, a new national development philosophy, and a new strategy for modernising the national governance system and governance capacity. The China story as commonly known is one of 'growth'. These transformations essentially involve the imagining and making of a 'post-growth' China.

From the early 2010s, China has been transitioning into a so-called 'new era' in terms of political leadership, modernisation discourse, and urban imaginary. China is trying to rewrite its growth story, departing from a focus on

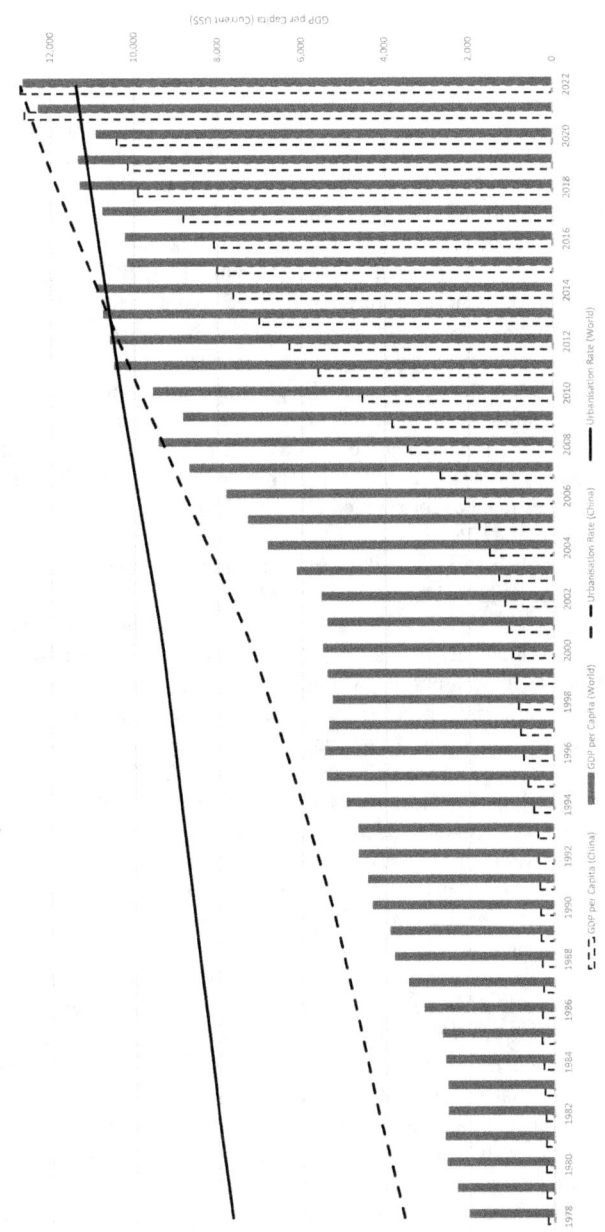

Figure 1.1 Urbanisation rate and GDP per capita: China versus the world, 1978–2022

Data source: The World Bank (2023a, 2023b), created by the author.

high-speed growth to a pursuit of 'high-quality development'. This quantity-quality shift underlies many aspects of the country's transformations in strategy and policy agendas.

In October 2017, at the 19th National Congress of the CPC, the most important political event for setting national development strategy, the principal contradiction confronting national development was reidentified as one of 'unbalanced and inadequate development versus the people's ever-growing needs for a better life' (Xu, 2017). Addressing this principal contradiction is expected to run through the whole process of China becoming a 'great modern socialist country' by the mid of the 21st century (Xu, 2017). Before that, China will achieve 'basic' modernisation by 2035 according to a roadmap outlined at this congress. As a result, the year 2035 has become a critical timeline in plan making, aligning urban plans with national development strategy. This new principal contradiction replaced the previous one of 'the ever-growing material and cultural needs of the people versus backward social production' (Xu, 2017), which was formalised in 1981 and had underpinned the drive for rapid growth for nearly four decades. This change of principal contradiction signified a strategic reorientation of national development, following the Marxist logic of the CPC.

Addressing the new principal contradiction requires a new development approach that is 'balanced' and 'adequate', filling the gaps between socioeconomic groups, between aspects of human wellbeing, and between regions. A set of new development notions—innovation, coordination, green, opening, and sharing—have been put in place in recent years, aspiring to sustainable development and common prosperity. As part of these broader development strategies and goals, China is pursuing a 'new-type urbanisation' that is human-centric and sustainable (Chinese Government, 2014).

In the official discourse, China is advancing the modernisation of its governance system and governance capacity. It is also exploring and promoting the so-called 'whole-process people's democracy' and deliberative democracy, a sort of Chinese democracy that is distinct from the Western one. Urban governance and regional governance are subordinate, integral, and contributory to this discourse of national governance and its goals.

'Chinese-style modernisation', an old notion revived in the new era, is now a buzzword in the official discourse after its formal endorsement at the 20th National Congress of the CPC held in October 2022. It is defined, sweepingly, as the modernisation 'of a huge population', 'of common prosperity for all', 'of material and cultural-ethical advancement', 'of harmony between humanity and nature', and 'of peaceful development' (Xi, 2022, pp. 18–19). It is the latest as well as the most authentic articulation of China's pursuit of modernisation in terms of vision, goals, and path.

China's urbanisation is integral to its modernisation. Of the major dimensions of China's transformative urbanisation is the rise of megaregions in the imagining, planning, and development of urban China.

Megaregions

Megaregions are the new form of China's urbanisation. Chinese cities are growing vertically and horizontally. Both densification and expansion characterise the change in their urban forms. Megaregionalisation, as the spatial representation of interlinked cities in terms of urban functions and connectivity, marks a critical stage of transformative urbanisation.

Megaregions are evolving in China and elsewhere. They stand out in China at the intersection of its rapid urbanisation and megaregionalisation, and at a critical time of its pursuit of high-quality, balanced, and sustainable development—all the hallmarks of the 'new-type urbanisation' being imagined and practised in China. These two interwoven transformative processes of urbanisation and megaregionalisation in the new development context call for new thinking and approaches to planning and governing megaregions.

The term megaregion has many equivalents, including megalopolis, mega city region, megapolitan region, and polyopolis. There is no standard definition of a megaregion. Definitions vary significantly, depending on contexts, perspectives, disciplines, and criteria. Generally, a megaregion is characterised by size, density, spread, polycentricity, complexity, and intraregional and interregional connectivity, forging an interconnected regionalised urban system. A definition of megaregions can be built upon a geospatial scale that delineates the territorial extent and boundary for regionalised functions and activities and enables arrangements for regionwide governance and policy and planning interventions.

Apart from the quantitative measures often used to define a megaregion, theorists tend to argue for the qualitatively different characteristics of it. A megaregion essentially refers to a polycentric urban agglomeration in terms of 'geographic proximity and functional connectivity' (Neuman & Hull, 2009, p. 777). It is emerging as a polycentric structure with internal specialisation (Hall, 2001), and as a political-economic unit with external and even extranational relationships (Scott, 2001). This urban-scale agglomeration has been mutually reinforced with a global-scale dispersion, technically enabled by improvements in transportation and communication conquering barriers of space and borders (Sassen, 2001; Scott, 2001).

To broadly summarise, a megaregion is—and can possibly be—characterised by multi-scalarity (local, regional, national, and global), multi-dimensionality (economical, political, spatial, social, cultural, and environmental), internal interaction and interdependence (economic collaboration and division of labour, commuting, and infrastructure), and external connectivity and global networks.

China is starting to define megaregions—geospatially, socioeconomically, and functionally—to inform its planning and governance approaches to integrated, coordinated regional development. These efforts, overall, are at an early stage and are of exploratory, experimental, and pioneering nature.

While some analogies can be drawn with international experiences, the scale and speed of the transformations in China's megaregions, coupled with its different political and socioeconomic contexts, attach many Chinese characteristics to its conceptualisation of and policy responses to megaregions.

Under the umbrella goal of achieving 'human-centric new-type urbanisation', the *14th Five-Year Plan* (2021–2025)—a strategic national development plan—outlines a spatial structure for China's urbanisation (Chinese Government, 2021). This spatial structure is established upon the megaregional concepts of 'city clusters' (*cheng shi qun*) and 'metropolitan circles' (*du shi quan*), respectively. These concepts underpin China's megaregional imaginary and planning.

City clusters

City cluster is not a new focus in the national policy, nor is it a new spatial form of China's urbanisation. Since the turn of the 21st century, relevant policies and initiatives have been growing along with the accelerated megaregionalisation. The trio of megaregions—the Beijing–Tianjin–Hebei region, Yangtze River delta region, and Pearl River delta region (or Greater Bay Area)—has received the most attention in policy making and scholarly debates. For a nationwide urban structure, the *13th Five-Year Plan* (2016–2020) first identified 19 city clusters. They are inherited in the latest *14th Five-Year Plan* (2021–2025). These city clusters constitute the strategic spatial structure for China's urban development. They forge a frame of 'two horizontals and three verticals' (*liang heng san zong*) that runs across mainly eastern and central China (Figure 1.2). This spatial structure is both indicative and imaginative about a megaregional China at present and in the future.

These 19 city clusters vary significantly by scale and stage of development. Apart from the well-known trio, some of them, which are mostly in mid-western China, are smaller and obscure in terms of size, influence, and economic strength. It is even questionable whether they should be called city clusters if the conventional definitions of megaregions are applied.

Metropolitan circles

Geospatially, a metropolitan circle is often smaller than, and lies within, a city cluster. Very often, metropolitan circles anchor city clusters. In China's urban policy documents, compared with the scoping of a city cluster that is indicative and generic, the definition and delineation of a metropolitan circle is specific and prescriptive.

A metropolitan circle is centred around a metropolitan centre—a central big city—and includes its surrounding smaller cities within a one-hour commuting circle. This definition was first put forward in the *National New-Type Urbanisation Plan* (2014–2020): 'The functions of metropolitan centres

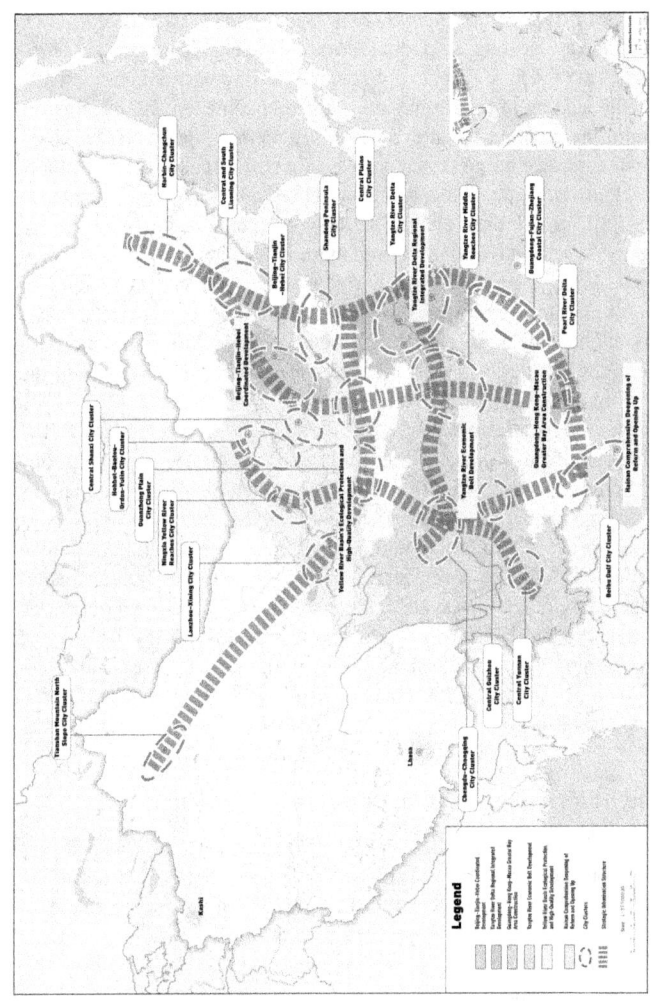

Figure 1.2 Spatial structure of megaregional China
Source: Chinese Government (2021), recreated by the author.

should radiate and spread into areas within one-hour transport, forging metropolitan circles with efficient commute and integrated development' (Chinese Government, 2014). The same definition is used in a series of relevant policy documents like the *Guiding Opinions on Cultivating and Developing Modern Metropolitan Circles* (2019), *14th Five-Year Plan* (2021–2025), and *Practical Codes for Territorial Spatial Planning of Metropolitan Circles* (2021).

Defining and delineating a metropolitan circle is a challenging task. Metropolitan circles are emerging and evolving; and they are interacting, internally and externally, adding to the complexity of the phenomenon and the elusiveness of capturing it. The official definition of a metropolitan circle based on the one-hour commute has practical problems in policy making and planning. It fails to acknowledge the diversity and variation of the numerous metropolitan circles in China. For example, the one-hour commute and its spatial scope in Beijing are significantly different from those in Nanjing, given the different sizes, population and built environment densities, and transport systems of these two cities. This one-hour commuting criterion for a metropolitan circle is seldom challenged since it is an 'official' definition used in the central government documents. In practice, this criterion is hardly observed in the planning for metropolitan circles (see Chapter 2).

Like city clusters, metropolitan circles are also of different sizes and at different stages of development. Most metropolitan circles are within one province. Some extend across provinces, like the Nanjing metropolitan circle that includes areas in both Jiangsu and Anhui provinces. There are also metropolitan circles that interlink and overlap, like the several metropolitan circles within the Yangtze River delta region, in which the Greater Shanghai metropolitan circle contains several constituent metropolitan circles (see Chapter 4). These multiple forms of metropolitan circles, while reflecting the dynamics of China's urbanisation and megaregionalisation, increase the challenges and complexities in defining them and adopting regional planning and governance responses.

The issue: Interregional and intraregional imbalances

> ... to consider megaregionalism in China for what it actually is: an always evolving political-economic project orchestrated by the CPC through a combination of spatial development strategies and urbanization policies to manage the complex relationship between increased exposure to external global capitalist market forces while maintaining tight authoritarian control over internal domestic matters.
>
> (Harrison & Gu, 2021, p. 78)

China's megaregions (and megacities) are one focus of global urban and regional studies. But to truly understand them is a challenge for interested observers. John Harrison and Hao Gu (2021) contend that there is no clear understanding of Chinese megaregionalism and propose the above assumption to debunk it. They team up to make commendable efforts 'to consider megaregionalism in China for what it actually is'. This assumption has its merits. It is right to consider megaregionalism in China—and in any country—as 'an always evolving political-economic project'. It is also right to understand the project as 'orchestrated by the CPC through a combination of spatial development strategies and urbanization policies to manage the complex relationship'. But the understanding of the complex relationship as 'between increased exposure to external global capitalist market forces while maintaining tight authoritarian control over internal domestic matters' is oversimplified, and there is a hint of stereotype in it. The 'complex relationship' should be plural, not singular. And this global-domestic binary is not at the centre of the complex relationships.

The central issue of megaregional China is the interregional and intraregional imbalances. This issue is well reflected in the above 'unbalanced and inadequate development' in the principal contradiction identified for China's development. There are clear disparities between megaregions in eastern coastal areas and those in mid-western inland areas. Within the same city cluster or metropolitan circle, intercity differences in terms of urbanisation rates and socioeconomic development are salient. The disparities are enlarging, not narrowing. Both interregional and intraregional imbalances will be further discussed in the subsequent chapters.

The interregional disparities explain why the mid-western megaregions (and cities) often set development goals of catching up with their eastern counterparts and propose strategies of learning from their best practices. These interregional benchmarking and diffusion in 'development planning', a sub-planning system in China (see Chapter 2), present an interesting dimension of China's interregional competition and collaboration. They could possibly become a channel for advancing innovative planning thinking and practice to address the unbalanced interregional development.

In an intraregional context, unbalanced development exists between cities, especially between the central city and the other member cities within a metropolitan circle. In terms of both population and GDP shares within a region, a common scenario is that the central city increases its shares while the other peripheral cities decrease theirs to various degrees. This growing 'centrality' of the central city exacerbates intraregional imbalances, countering the policy intention of rebalancing intercity disparities.

However, the degree of imbalances differs by megaregions. Overall, intraregional development is more balanced in eastern areas than in mid-western areas. The least developed megaregions—often in the most western areas—have the most unbalanced intercity development within themselves. These megaregions confront dual challenges in regional development: externally, they need to catch up with their eastern developed counterparts; internally, they need to address the escalating intercity imbalances.

These interregional and intraregional imbalances and their nuances in different regional contexts reinforce the necessity for integrated, coordinated regional development, and for planning and governance interventions to achieve it.

The imperative: From fragmentation to collaboration

Fragmentation characterises megaregional governance in China and elsewhere. In China, it materialises in terms of 'jurisdictional fragmentation' (Yeh & Chen, 2020, p. 636); it also materialises in terms of 'state-centric skewed governance, political competition among local governments and inter-ministry rivalries', which complicate power interplay in regional institution and regional cooperation (Dai et al., 2014, p. 433). However, intergovernmental relationship presents only a partial picture of the problem, despite being the most important aspect of the problem. Fragmentation in megaregional governance involves both governmental and nongovernmental actors.

China's megaregional governance is centred around achieving integrated development across a megaregion through coordination and deliberation between governments—vertical and horizontal—and between multiple stakeholders—public, private, and community. To date, intergovernmental collaboration and multistakeholder participation have been fragmented, competitive, conflicted, insufficient, or missing. The imperative for megaregional governance is to enable such collaboration and participation to achieve consensus-based envisioning, policy making, and planning, and further, concerted actions to achieve integrated, balanced regional development, as aspired to in vision, imagining, and agenda setting.

Regardless of the technical criteria and measurement, the Chinese definition of a megaregion is built upon a territorial scope containing member cities that are geographically and functionally interlinked but administratively separated. This definition presents the geospatial base as well as the core problem in tackling megaregional governance—the governance of several or a group of cities within a region.

To better understand megaregional governance in the Chinese context, it is important to know what it is not about:

First, megaregional governance is not about metropolitan governance. The concepts of 'megaregional governance' and 'metropolitan governance' are differentiated to reflect the particular use of the former in the Chinese context. The geographical scope of megaregional governance is the whole megaregion that contains its member cities. The geographical scope of metropolitan governance is the administrative area of a metropolis—a provincial-level, sub-provincial-level, or prefecture-level city (see below and Chapter 2 for their differences)—that contains its urban districts and rural surrounds.

For example, the 'Hangzhou metropolitan circle governance' covers Hangzhou and its surrounding cities like Shaoxing, Jiaxing, Huzhou, and Quzhou in Zhejiang province, and even Huangshan in Anhui province (see also Chapter 4). The 'Hangzhou metropolitan governance' simply covers the geographical and administrative area of Hangzhou city. Reflecting this difference, metropolitan circle governance concerns regionwide matters across several jurisdictions, while metropolitan governance concerns only one city-level jurisdiction.

Second, megaregional governance is not about megaregional government. There is not a level of megaregional government in the Chinese administrative system. Largely because of this, megaregional governance becomes problematic. However, governance is not about government only: megaregional governance involves governmental and nongovernmental stakeholders, both of which are inside the megaregion; the stakeholders are also outside the megaregion—like higher-level governments or external investors. Governance is sometimes equated with government, mistakenly, in discussing megaregional governance in the Chinese context.

Without doubt, governments are the most important stakeholders in China's megaregional governance. In a metropolitan circle, horizontally, there are governments of constituent cities; vertically, there are governments at all administrative levels from the central government to grassroots governments. Within the Chinese administrative system, the member cities of a metropolitan circle are prefecture-level cities (PLCs) (*di ji shi*), which are under the provincial government and then the highest central government, and which are above urban districts, counties, or county-level cities (see also Chapter 3).

As of the end of 2022, there were 293 PLCs within provinces and 40 equivalents of PLCs in autonomous regions in China (Ministry of Civil Affairs, 2022). Across the country, under the central government there are 23 provinces, five autonomous regions, four provincial-level municipalities or direct-administered municipalities (see Chapter 2), and two special administrative regions of Hong Kong and Macau. Thus, the PLCs—the middle level in the Chinese administrative system—are the major jurisdictions as well as government stakeholders in a megaregion.

In theory, the member cities of a metropolitan circle are at the same administrative level as PLCs, granting them equal status. However, of the 293 PLCs, 15 are classified as so-called sub-provincial-level cities (*fu sheng ji shi*). These sub-provincial-level cities are not at a higher administrative level than PLCs per se, but their top leaders are appointed at the sub-provincial-level and are managed by the central government (see also Chapter 3). The existence of sub-provincial-level cities creates unequal status—and sometimes confusion—among member cities of a metropolitan circle, although they all are PLCs.

Several fundamental notions underpin an understanding of and approaches to collaborative governance for megaregions. They can be summarised as follows:

First, the government-market relationality levers collaborative megaregional governance. Megaregions are outcomes of a natural, spontaneous process that is more market-driven than government-led. The premise of collaborative governance is to recognise the role of market forces in driving regional development. It is of crucial importance to balance the market-government relationality in comprehending and forming collaborative governance for megaregions.

Second, collaborative megaregional governance is more than intergovernmental collaboration. It is about engaging all stakeholders in a genuinely participatory and communicative process of deliberation and coordination. A government-centric notion of governance tends to focus on intergovernmental collaboration between member cities within a megaregion, impacting the incorporation of nongovernmental stakeholders, and further impacting the inclusion of non-public contribution, innovation, and ingenuity into collaborative megaregional governance.

Third, collaborative megaregional governance is voluntary, deliberative, and coordinative. Collaborative megaregional governance is nothing mandatory. It is about building partnerships among stakeholders through negotiation and agreement to achieve a win-win scenario of 'co-developing' (*gong jian*), 'sharing' (*gong xiang*), and 'co-governing' (*gong zhi*) a megaregion (NDRC, 2019). There is no panacea or one-size-fits-all model of collaborative governance: it is very important to combine best practice principles with local settings to develop bespoke approaches that are authentic, adaptive, and resilient.

Overview and organisation of the book

This introductory Chapter 1 sets the contexts and defines the concepts for understanding megaregional China and raises the issue of regional imbalances and the imperative for collaborative megaregional governance. The Chinese-style urbanisation is taking a new form of megaregionalisation. Megaregions forge the spatial structure for China's pursuit of 'high-quality development' and 'new-type urbanisation'—the key notions and goals in China's new development strategy and urban transformation. There are two concepts—'city cluster' and 'metropolitan circle'—in China's discourse of megaregional planning and governance. These concepts both clarify and confuse in theory and practice: they are evolving conceptually and are being tested practically. The chapter captures the central issue of interregional and intraregional imbalances, aligning regional development with national development through the principal contradiction that underpins the reorientation of China's development in philosophy, vision, and strategy. Critically, the chapter argues that the imperative for China's megaregional governance is to transform from fragmentation to collaboration to achieve integrated, balanced regional development. Both the issue and the imperative shape the planning and governance of megaregional China and determine the success or failure of them.

Chapter 2 examines the latest planning system and practice for megaregions in China. China has just completed a comprehensive reform of its planning system. However, this new system still has a grey area for regional planning. A regional plan has neither a statutory status nor a corresponding administrative level for its making, management, and implementation. Largely for these reasons, a regional plan is essentially an 'articulator' plan—articulating plans of various types and at various levels. In planning for megaregions, the Chinese government has set nuanced goals for city clusters and metropolitan circles: 'integrated development' for the former and 'one-city development' for the latter. Both broad goals are centred on coordinating the planning of a megaregion that is unbalanced and fragmented into one that is balanced and collaborative. To illustrate these, the chapter discusses the latest planning for the Beijing–Tianjin–Hebei region and the Chengdu metropolitan circle, respectively. Under a strong political will and a belief in 'top-level design', these regional imaginaries present challenges in terms of sustaining long-term implementation and articulating with other plans for these megaregions.

Chapter 3 delves into three major development areas of metropolitan circles: economic development, connectivity, and investment. For each of the areas, the chapter presents national contexts and policies, analyses regional practices, and critically reveals the problems and challenges and the root causes for them. Collaborative economic development in a metropolitan circle involves not only intercity collaboration but also balancing the government-market relationality. A government-led approach to the planning and development of the regional economy often fails to engage the market actors of enterprises and entrepreneurs. In understanding regional connectivity of a metropolitan circle, it is important to differentiate between transport and transit and prioritise the latter over the former in thinking and practice. This suggests an imperative for improving the 'soft power' of transport planning and governance to match the 'hard power' of transport infrastructure construction. Investment underlies any area of development for a metropolitan circle. But a fundamental contradiction lies between governments horizontally and vertically. In policy debates and advocacy, emphasis has been laid on intergovernmental co-funding in projects of regional importance. However, the vertical intergovernmental imbalance between financial powers and financial responsibilities is the prime barrier to regional investment. There is no easy solution to any of these problems or challenges. They require both top-down policy design and bottom-up ingenuity to achieve 'one-city development' for metropolitan circles.

Chapter 4 dissects the multi-scalar spatial imaginary and planning across the Yangtze River delta that involve both top-down envisioning and bottom-up initiatives. Bold imaginary is proposed for various regional scales, but they each confront prominent issues. The whole Yangtze River delta region is an administrative delineation that includes three provinces—Zhejiang, Jiangsu, and Anhui—and one provincial-level municipality Shanghai. Within this region, both interprovincial and intraprovincial imbalances in socioeconomic development exist. The Yangtze River delta city cluster is a city region of national leadership and global influence. This city cluster contains several metropolitan circles that are not spatially distinct but rather interlinked, defying the conventional definition of metropolitan circles by a commuting range. For Shanghai, the dragon's head in the region, a Greater Shanghai metropolitan circle is being imagined, extending into neighbouring provinces, cities, and metropolitan circles. These complexities in the spatial imaginary for the Yangtze River delta reflect, on the one hand, the increasingly mingled megaregionalisation and urbanisation. On the other hand, they demand strategic and innovative megaregional planning response and intervention. However, the surging regional plans—both top-down and bottom-up—share a common issue of imaginary-practice gap.

Chapter 5 unravels the relational planning between Shenzhen and Hong Kong in the Greater Bay Area. These two cities have a unique relationality under China's governance structure of 'one country, two systems'. Both the intercity relationality and 'one country, two systems' are shifting at an accelerating pace over the recent decade, and especially in recent years after the 2019 street movement in Hong Kong. In terms of relational planning, the previous Hong Kong-led 'internationalisation' of Shenzhen is being replaced by the Shenzhen-led 'nationalisation' of Hong Kong, as observed in the evolving strategic plans and spatial imaginaries of the two cities. The underlying factors are multi-scalar: intercity, regional, national, and international; they are also complicated, involving relational shifts in economic power and associated social, political, and cultural changes between Hong Kong and Shenzhen (and further the Greater Bay Area and the mainland). Chinese traditional wisdom of *yin-yang* sheds light on the relational planning and the relational shifts between the two cities. In both the national and international contexts, the Greater Bay Area presents a unique case of exploring, innovating, and experimenting with megaregional planning and governance. This uniqueness is the most represented by the Shenzhen–Hong Kong relationality in terms of 'one country, two cities'.

References

Chinese Government. (2014). *National new-type urbanisation plan (2014–2020)*. [in Chinese]. http://www.gov.cn/zhengce/2014-03/16/content_2640075.htm

Chinese Government. (2021). *The People's Republic of China's 14th five-year plan for national economic and social development and outline objectives of the 2035 vision.* [in Chinese]. NDRC. http://www.gov.cn/xinwen/2021-03/13/content_5592681.htm

Dai, L., Sit, V. F.-S., & Li, G. (2014). Decoding regional cooperation and governance in Central China: A case study in the Chang-Zhu-Tan urban cluster. *Town Planning Review*, 85(4), 433–456. https://doi.org/10.3828/tpr.2014.24

Hall, P. (2001). Global city regions in the twenty-first century. In A. J. Scott (Ed.), *Global city-regions: Trends, theory, policy* (pp. 59–77). Oxford University Press.

Hamadeh, N., Rompaey, C. V., & Metreau, E. (2023, 30 June). *World Bank Group country classifications by income level for FY24 (July 1, 2023–June 30, 2024)*. World Bank Blogs. https://blogs.worldbank.org/opendata/new-world-bank-group-country-classifications-income-level-fy24

Harrison, J., & Gu, H. (2021). Planning megaregional futures: Spatial imaginaries and megaregion formation in China. *Regional Studies, 55*(1), 77–89. https://doi.org/10.1080/00343404.2019.1679362

Ministry of Civil Affairs. (2022, 31 December). *An inventory of administrative divisions of the People's Republic of China*. [in Chinese]. http://xzqh.mca.gov.cn/statistics/2022.html

NDRC (National Development and Reform Commission). (2019). *Guiding opinions on cultivating and developing modern metropolitan circles*. [in Chinese]. www.gov.cn/xinwen/2019-02/21/content_5367465.htm

Neuman, M., & Hull, A. (2009). The future of the city region. *Regional Studies, 43*(6), 777–787.

Sassen, S. (2001). Global cities and global city regions: A comparison. In A. J. Scott (Ed.), *Global city-regions: Trends, theory, policy* (pp. 78–95). Oxford University Press.

Scott, A. J. (Ed.). (2001). *Global city-regions: Trends, theory, policy*. Oxford University Press.

The World Bank. (2023a). *GDP per capita (current US$)*. https://data.worldbank.org/indicator/NY.GDP.PCAP.CD

The World Bank. (2023b). *Urban population (% of total population)*. https://data.worldbank.org/indicator/SP.URB.TOTL.IN.ZS

United Nations. (2018). *World urbanization prospects: The 2018 revision*. Department of Economic and Social Affairs, Population Division. https://population.un.org/wup/Country-Profiles/

Xi, J. (2022, 25 October). *Hold high the great banner of socialism with Chinese characteristics and strive in unity to build a modern socialist country in all respects*. Xinhuanet. https://english.news.cn/20221025/8eb6f5239f984f01a2bc45b5b5db0c51/c.html

Xu, L. (2017, 20 October). *Xinhua insight: China embraces new 'principal contradiction' when embarking on new journey*. Xinhuanet. http://www.xinhuanet.com/english/2017-10/20/c_136694592.htm

Yeh, A. G.-O., & Chen, Z. (2020). From cities to super mega city regions in China in a new wave of urbanisation and economic transition: Issues and challenges. *Urban Studies, 57*(3), 636–654. https://doi.org/10.1177/0042098019879566

2 Planning megaregions

Tianjin is known for its humorous local culture. It is where the comic dialogue (*xiang sheng*) originated and flourishes. In those years after the September 11 attacks in 2001, there was a popular joke, which was said to be invented by Tianjiners:

> Osama bin Laden's plane was flying over China to target a Chinese city. When it was above Shanghai, Laden was impressed by the city's glamour and prosperity, and he changed his mind. When it was above Beijing, he was impressed by the city's historic and scenic places of interest, and he changed his mind again. When it was above Tianjin, his aide suggested that this was China's third greatest city after Beijing and Shanghai only. Laden looked down and was puzzled, 'Didn't we just bombard it?'

The humorous Tianjiners made fun of their home city's slow growth and change compared with its counterpart tier-one cities in China. That was 20 years ago. Today, Tianjin is not comparable even with some tier-two Chinese cities in terms of urban development and economic growth.

Four Chinese cities—Beijing, Tianjin, Shanghai, and Chongqing—are so-called direct-administered municipalities (DAMs) (*zhi xia shi*). As cities, they have the same rank as provinces—for this reason, they are provincial-level municipalities—and are directly under the central government in China's administrative hierarchy. The DAM status reflects their importance in China's socioeconomic development and governance system. Politically, they are even more important than many provinces. The incumbent Politburo of the Communist Party of China (CPC)—the central organ of decision making for the party and the country—was established in October 2022. Its 24 members include all the party secretaries of the four DAMs. But for provinces, its membership includes only the party secretaries of Guangdong and Xinjiang—a province and a provincial-level autonomous region, respectively. The remaining members are all heads of central government agencies. This convention of appointing provincial-level leaders into the top decision-making organ has been followed in recent decades. This reflects a political recognition of the

DOI: 10.4324/9781003108405-2

importance of these DAMs—and of megacities in general—in China's political power structure.

These four DAMs have achieved this status for well-justified historical and contemporary reasons. Beijing is the national capital. Shanghai is a prime economic centre. Chongqing was created as a DAM in 1997 to drive Western Development—the campaign for developing western China—and to coordinate the relocation of more than one million residents to vacate the territory for the forthcoming Three Gorges Dam, the world's largest power station project. Tianjin was an important port city in northern China in history. In much of the first half of the 20th century, like Shanghai and several other Chinese cities that had foreign concessions, Tianjin was also a prime economic centre and China's gateway to modernity. But the city's development and status in both the regional and the national urban systems have triggered considerable debates in recent years. These debates have significant implications for the planning of the Beijing–Tianjin–Hebei region.

In 2022, the top ten Chinese cities in the mainland by aggregate gross domestic product (GDP) were Shanghai, Beijing, Shenzhen, Chongqing, Guangzhou, Suzhou, Chengdu, Wuhan, Hangzhou, and Nanjing. Tianjin was eased out of this list by those southern cities. Tianjin is only 130 km away from Beijing, a commute of 1.5 hours by car on expressway or 30 minutes by train on high-speed rail (HSR). In the several years of the late 1980s and early 1990s, when expressways were a rarity in mainland China, these two cities were connected by one of the earliest expressways; this expressway was textbook knowledge for students of geography then. However, despite the proximity and connectivity between them, Beijing and Tianjin are not twin cities. They are distinct in terms of political status and, because of this, they are distinct in terms of resources, influence, competitiveness, and attractiveness.

Geospatially, Tianjin is better positioned than Beijing for a city's development. It is coastal and has port facilities, natural endowments that Beijing envies, but Beijing has the most enviable asset for any Chinese city—it is the national capital. It is tempting to ask these questions:

- What would Tianjin be like if it were not so close to Beijing?
- Would Tianjin's development be better than it is today?
- Is Beijing a blessing or a curse for Tianjin?

The assumption that having a giant neighbour is a disadvantage for a city's development is refuted by Suzhou, which is even closer to Shanghai than Tianjin is to Beijing. Suzhou has benefited so much from the spillovers of Shanghai, presenting a different development trajectory from that of Tianjin.

In the recent decade, great imaginings and efforts have been made to rebalance the development of the Beijing–Tianjin–Hebei region, which has been elevated as a national strategy. Similar planning efforts have also been made for other megaregions, like the Yangtze River delta region and the Greater Bay Area; the development of each of them has also been endorsed as a national strategy. China is in an age of megaregional planning.

Regional planning system

China has recently reformed its planning system. My book *Reinventing the Chinese City* (2023) introduces this reform and the new planning system (Hu, 2023, pp. 199–205). Here, I briefly recap them and discuss the relevance to regional planning.

Over several decades, 'integrating multiple plans into one' (*duo gui he yi*) has been the key notion in major debates on reforming the planning system. The debates have focused on how to establish 'one' planning system, replacing the previous 'multiple' systems and plans that were deemed to be fragmented, confusing, and conflicting.

Since early 2018, the Chinese government has undertaken the most comprehensive planning system reform. In that year, it created a new Ministry of Natural Resources (MNR) to oversee a renamed 'territorial spatial planning' (*guo tu kong jian gui hua*) system that integrates multiple spatial plans. Previously, these spatial plans belonged to separate planning systems and were responsibilities of different government agencies, creating disconnection and inconsistency between them. The new territorial spatial planning system is essentially about 'spatial planning', despite some elaborations on the nuances between them in the Chinese planning discourse. This territorial spatial planning system started to be implemented in May 2019.

In addition, China also has a development planning system that has been in use since the 1950s, a legacy of the Soviet planning's influence at that time. It is mainly about making and endorsing strategic plans for economic and social development. A typical such plan is the five-year plan, like the latest *14th Five-Year Plan* (2021–2025).

Thus, the new Chinese planning system contains two subsystems: a development planning system and a territorial spatial planning system (see Figure 2.1). These planning systems interconnect, broadly and loosely. They are still responsibilities of different government agencies. At the national level, the National Development and Reform Commission (NDRC) takes charge of the development planning, and the new MNR leads the territorial spatial planning. At lower-level governments, their subordinate agencies—the development and reform commission and the bureau of natural resources—oversee the two planning systems, respectively.

The new planning system structures plan types in alignment with administrative levels, ranging from the national level to the grassroots level of township/town (Figure 2.1). Regional planning often involves several

Planning megaregions 19

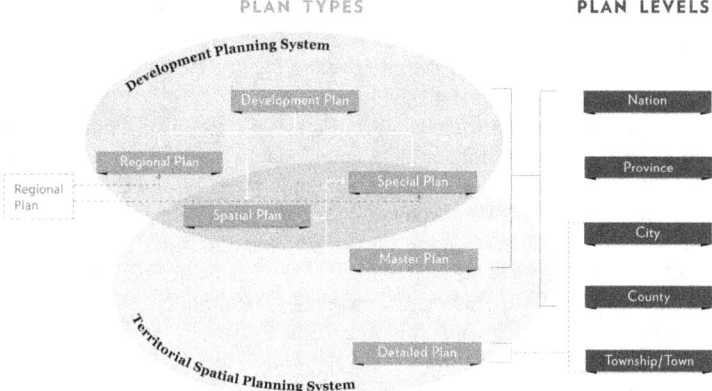

Figure 2.1 Regional plan in the new Chinese planning system
Source: The author.

administrative units, large or small. Consequently, a regional plan is not aligned to any administrative level in this structure. As a plan type, it sits within both the development planning system and the territorial spatial planning system—it is a 'regional plan' in the former system and a 'special plan' in the latter system—without corresponding to a plan level (Figure 2.1). This situation creates a grey area for regional planning.

No matter how it is labelled in the Chinese planning system, a regional plan is an 'articulator' plan—articulating between the higher-level national or provincial plans and the lower-level plans of cities/counties within a region. A regional plan has no statutory status in either the development planning system or the territorial spatial planning system. This lack of clearly-defined standing and a statutory status in the planning system creates confusion, uncertainty, ambiguity, and paradox in the making and governance of a regional plan, and further in its articulation with plans of various types and at different levels. These problems apply to planning for both city clusters and metropolitan circles—the two key megaregional scales in China's urban structure (see Chapter 1).

Integrated development for city clusters

According to the *14th Five-Year Plan* (2021–2025), the central goal of planning city clusters is to achieve 'integrated development' (*yi ti hua fa zhan*) for each of them through the establishment of regional coordination systems, sharing of development costs and benefits, holistic infrastructure planning and construction, collaborative industrial development and division of labour, sharing of public services, and co-protection and co-governance of ecological environment (Chinese Government, 2021). In these areas, the city clusters are not yet 'integrated' across their member cities that are spatially and functionally connected but administratively distinct.

Unsurprisingly, the trio of city clusters—the Beijing–Tianjin–Hebei region, Yangtze River delta region, and Greater Bay Area—has attracted the most attention in policy making, academic research, and media reportage. This trio, as of 2015, accounted for 5 per cent of the national land, but 24 per cent of its population, and 40 per cent of its GDP (Yeh & Chen, 2020, p. 637). They are the backbones of China's urbanisation and the engines of its economic growth. They are also important regional nodes of the global urban system, underpinning China's connection with the world. Like other megaregions at home and elsewhere, they also confront common planning issues of regional coordination and integration. However, each of them has its own geospatial, environmental, socioeconomical, and political contexts that characterise its patterns of urbanisation and regional development. There has been no shortage of regional planning initiatives and imaginings for each of them since the turn of the century. Despite the mixed outcomes of these plans of various types, they have at least enhanced an awareness of the importance of regional planning for these megaregions.

In the recent decade, the central government has employed a more proactive and interventionist approach to the planning of these megaregions (see Table 2.1). Recent regional plans for them produced by the central government include the *Outline Plan for Coordinated Development of the Beijing–Tianjin–Hebei Region* (2015), *Development Plan for the Yangtze River Delta City Cluster* (2016), *Outline Plan for Integrated Development of the Yangtze River Delta Region* (2019), and *Outline Plan for Development of the Guangdong–Hong Kong–Macau Greater Bay Area* (2019). All the outline plans were released by the Central Committee of the CPC and the State Council, signalling the political importance attached to these plans and the development of these regions.

The making of the development plans for these megaregions was led by the NDRC, the central government agency that has the most planning power, especially in the development planning system discussed earlier. For its overall planning power, the NDRC is often dubbed as 'little State Council'. The NDRC was previously called National Planning Commission. The current name was adopted in 1998 to reflect the national shift from a planned economy to a market economy and the agency's focus on development and reform matters rather than 'planning', a term reminiscent of the Maoist era. However, the NDRC remains the most powerful agency for national planning of socioeconomic development. This includes the development planning for megaregions that often spread across several provinces.

Table 2.1 Planning the trio of city clusters

	Beijing–Tianjin–Hebei region	Yangtze River delta region	Greater Bay Area
Land area	216,000 km²	211,700 km²	56,000 km²
Population	110 million	150 million	86 million
GDP	RMB 8.5 trillion	RMB 12.67 trillion	RMB 12.02 trillion
Recent regional plans	*Outline Plan for Coordinated Development of the Beijing–Tianjin–Hebei Region* (2015)	*Development Plan for the Yangtze River Delta City Cluster* (2016) *Outline Plan for Integrated Development of the Yangtze River Delta Region* (2019)	*Outline Plan for Development of the Guangdong–Hong Kong–Macau Greater Bay Area* (2019)
Key regional planning issues	• Overdominance of Beijing in the region • Beijing's 'big city syndrome'	• International competitiveness of Shanghai and the region • Intraregional and urban–rural imbalances	• 'One country, two systems' • Belt and Road Initiative • Challenging and uncertain international situations
Major regional development objectives	• To alleviate the pressures of Beijing's non-capital functions • To achieve coordinated and balanced regional development	• To build a world-class city cluster with global influence • To achieve integrated regional development	• To build an international bay area and a world-class city cluster • To build an innovation-led economic system and development model

Reimagining the Beijing–Tianjin–Hebei region

In Chapters 4 and 5, I will discuss the planning and development issues in the Yangtze River delta region and the Greater Bay Area, respectively. Here, I focus on the Beijing–Tianjin–Hebei region. Altogether, Beijing, Tianjin, and Hebei province have a land area of 216,000 km², and they had a total population of 110 million and regional GDP of RMB 8.5 trillion as of 2018 (Table 2.1); these accounted for 2.3 per cent, 8.1 per cent, and 9.4 per cent in the national aggregates, respectively (NDRC, 2019a). In many aspects of regional development, like economic strength, global competitiveness, and marketisation of economic sectors, this region is lagging behind its southern counterparts. Its regional development issues, especially in terms of intraregional imbalances, are the most acute and complicated among the trio of city clusters.

Hebei province probably sits in the most awkward position in the map of China's political-economic geography. It is a coastal province: this is not a familiar perception for many Chinese, however; they will think about it for several seconds if they are asked about it. Hebei's modest coastline along the inlet of Bohai Bay has not brought the economic opportunities those southern coastal provinces have enjoyed. Within its territory, it contains two DAMs. Intuitively, these geospatial endowments can be seen as a blessing for the province. However, many Hebei residents may disagree. The province does not seem to have benefited from its proximity to the two DAMs, while the southern provinces, like Guangdong and Jiangsu, have clearly capitalised on the spill-overs of neighbouring megacities. For a long time, Hebei has been perceived as the province that has made sacrifices for the national capital's development in terms of provision of water and environmental resources and loss of socioeconomic development opportunities. Ironically and worryingly, some Hebei counties bordering Beijing and Tianjin suffer from poverty, forging a 'poverty belt' (*ping kun dai*) surrounding the two megacities. This contrast is described metaphorically as 'European city surrounded by African countryside' (SCMP Reporter, 2006).

The intraregional imbalances are epitomised by the overconcentration of growth and resources in Beijing in contrast with—and at the cost of—its neighbouring cities. The reasons are complicated and have historical roots. The emergence of the Beijing–Tianjin–Hebei region is more an outcome of political factors than market forces. The regional economy has a higher share of state-owned enterprises (SOEs)—implying a lower marketisation level—than the national average (Song, 2017, p. 4). Those provinces in southern China—including Guangdong, Zhejiang, and Jiangsu—that have benefited from the agglomeration economies of megaregions are also known for their high marketisation levels and dynamic private sectors in the provincial economies. Market forces enable and lubricate regional collaboration and spillovers. On the contrary, some places in the 'poverty belt' in Hebei are restricted in local economic development out of administrative and military controls for their proximity to the national capital in addition to the unfavourable geographical and climatic settings. While Beijing is growing bigger and bigger, its divide with other cities in the region is becoming wider and wider, exacerbating intraregional imbalances.

Unbalanced development has been a concern for the Beijing–Tianjin–Hebei region for some time. What has been more a concern is probably the 'big city syndrome' that Beijing has been suffering. Many Chinese cities confront contemporary urban challenges and problems of various types and to various degrees, but Beijing is the most frequently quoted case of 'big city syndrome'. Since the turn of the century, air pollution, heavy traffic, low quality of life, and unsustainability have become new calling cards of the national capital. Wanton and ill-planned growth has created problems that seem to go beyond the city's capacity to address.

The central government has endorsed the strongest intervention into the regional planning of the Beijing–Tianjin–Hebei region in the recent decade, largely driven by Xi Jinping's personal interest and political will. The central tenet is to alleviate Beijing of its non-capital functions and relocate them elsewhere in the region. This has the dual aims of reducing Beijing's population density and achieving balanced regional development.

In 2013–2017, Xi Jinping visited sites in the region and gave a series of directives on coordinated development of it (Song, 2017, p. 5). In June 2014, the central government established the Leadership Group for Coordinated Development of the Beijing–Tianjin–Hebei Region, a high-profile group headed by the deputy premier in office, to oversee the regional planning and development. This was an exceptional high-level arrangement advocated presumably by Xi Jinping. This top-down approach has followed so-called 'top-level design' (*ding ceng she ji*), a notion proposed and promoted for strategic policy making and governance since late 2012 when Xi Jinping and a new generation of leaders came into power. In those years after the leadership group was established, several strategic meetings were held at the central government level, discussing and approving initiatives of coordinated development for the region. These initiatives involve regional governance and policy issues, like an integrated regional market for production factors, integrated reforms for public services, and regional development mechanisms and systems.

But the most prominent initiatives are two plans for building new cities to relocate Beijing's non-capital functions there. One plan is for building a Beijing subcentre. The idea of building a subcentre for Beijing to alleviate the overcrowding in the central city area had been on and off for some years. In 2015–2016, the idea was formalised and endorsed by the central government as part of the national strategy for coordinated development of the Beijing–Tianjin–Hebei region. The Beijing subcentre was designated in Tongzhou district to the east of central Beijing. Tongzhou is an existing urban centre in metropolitan Beijing. Building it into the Beijing subcentre did not have to start from scratch in terms of urban development, but the initiative has significantly enhanced its importance in metropolitan Beijing and the Beijing–Tianjin–Hebei region. The Beijing subcentre is a new civic centre for accommodating the Beijing municipal government and its agencies and associated resources, which are being relocated there from central Beijing. With this relocation, central Beijing is dedicated exclusively to holding the central government agencies and functions, fulfilling Beijing's role as the national capital only. In January 2019, the Beijing municipal government formally moved into the Beijing subcentre. Both the construction of the civic centre and the movement of other municipal agencies are still ongoing. Without doubt, these are reshaping Beijing's urban structure.

The relocation of the Beijing municipal government out of central Beijing and the construction of a new civic centre to accommodate it are

24 Planning megaregions

a bold endeavour. An even bolder endeavour is to build a new city from scratch in a vast rural land with a water system. This is the Xiong'an New Area, which was announced on 1 April 2017. Xiong'an sits in Hebei province to the south of Beijing. Geographically, it is in the geometrical centre of the major cities in the region, but the site itself is in the middle of nowhere (Figure 2.2). Xiong'an is intended to accommodate those non-capital functions to be relocated out of central Beijing. The planning of Xiong'an has been completed, and it is in the early stage of infrastructure construction and urban development. Several Beijing-based SOEs and universities are going to build subsidiaries or campuses there, according to public reportage. But, as of January 2024, no substantial action or presence of them has been observed except for buildings under construction or sites delineated.

Xiong'an has stimulated romantic imaginings about China's 'new-type urbanisation', like green, smart, sustainable, human-centric, and liveable—exactly the opposites of Beijing's 'big city syndrome'. But it has also raised criticism and doubt, justifying the 'Xiong'an paradox' in terms of its feasibility and sustainability (Hu, 2020, pp. 151–153). Indeed, Xiong'an is Xi Jinping's city-making project. Official reportage stresses that Xi proposed the idea and made the decision. The imagining of building such a new city in the middle of nowhere is more a political will than a pragmatic reasoning. It is a state project and does not seem to have engaged market forces. Since its

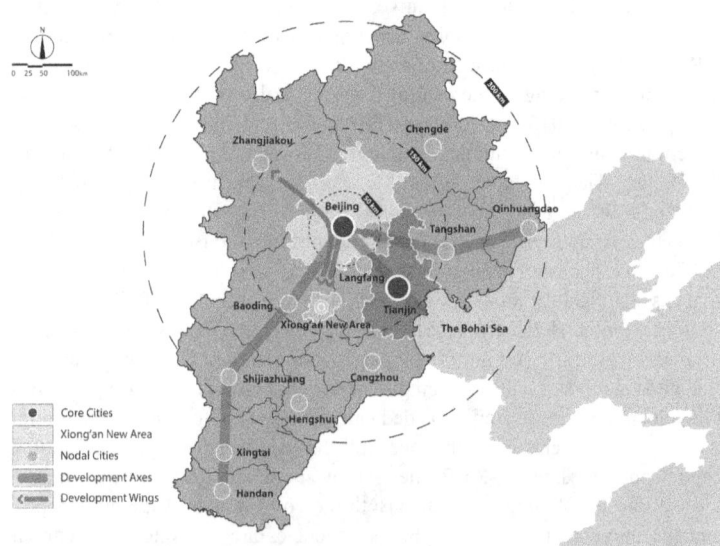

Figure 2.2 Beijing–Tianjin–Hebei region

Source: Hebei Government (2018), recreated by the author.

announcement in 2017, no sign has shown that this is a city that would grow organically and naturally by itself if it were not for the state machine driving its planning, investment, and construction.

It is tempting to compare Xiong'an with Shenzhen and Pudong, all of which are signature new cities made in China (Hu, 2020, pp. 135–154). People tend to use the success of Shenzhen and Pudong to allude to the likely success of Xiong'an. Official reportage assumes that Xiong'an will be even more successful than its predecessors, praising the wise decision of Xi Jinping.

This may not be a good comparison, however. Xiong'an differs from Shenzhen and Pudong in terms of vision, timing, and geographical location. Endowed geographical locations—Shenzhen is close to Hong Kong and Pudong is part of Shanghai—and market forces have played critical roles in growing them into leading economic centres. Xiong'an has neither the geographical location nor the market forces that its predecessors could access but political will and state investment. Political will also played important roles in the genesis and early development of both Shenzhen and Pudong. Deng Xiaoping used them to spearhead his 'reform and opening-up' agenda. However, the rapid growth of them into urban centres of international leadership has benefited the most from market forces at home and overseas. State investment had played a limited role in the growth of them; the government simply had no money to invest in them in the early stage of their development.

Xiong'an is not imagined as another economic centre like Shenzhen or Pudong, but as a location for accommodating those non-capital functions from Beijing. However, the relocation of those non-capital functions—if this is going to happen at a considerable scale—is not a result of spill-overs from Beijing driven by market forces, but rather one of administrative order through government intervention. Many public agencies must be relocated to Xiong'an, willingly or unwillingly, as an imposed top-down decision. There have been rumours that some Beijing-based agencies have been reluctant to move when directed to do so. The removal of the Beijing government agencies out of the central city area to Tongzhou district—the Beijing subcentre now—was also a proposal contested for years. It was the firm intervention from the central government and Xi Jinping's political will that made it happen. Presumably, the relocation of those non-capital functions from Beijing to Xiong'an will be a testing and contesting experience for individual agencies and their personnel. In the early growth of both Shenzhen and Pudong, the spill-overs from their neighbouring urban centres were voluntary, natural, and market-based. Xiong'an seems to be the opposite.

In its imagining, future Xiong'an will be a city with a population of five million (Hu, 2023, p. 147). The idea of building such a big city largely through government intervention and investment is more than bold; it is utopian.

Utopianism is not a rarity in Chinese urban imaginary. The critical prism to the future of Xiong'an is the government-market relationality—how a government-backed initiative will sustain a new city's growth, which will have to be tested by the market in the long run.

The Beijing–Tianjin–Hebei region is Beijing-centric (see Figure 2.2). Geospatially, this pattern counters the natural evolutions of many megaregions that are coastal. The emergence of this region has not been natural, however. Its regional planning approach intends to counter the centripetal forces of Beijing to rebalance regional development—a centrifugal process. Both centripetal and centrifugal forces are at play in negotiating the coordinated development of the region. Government intervention has made Beijing's dominance in the region. Now government intervention is trying to mitigate its dominance.

Sometimes, the Chinese official rhetoric has an admirable capacity of creating new terms. 'Reduction-based development' (*jian liang fa zhan*), literally an oxymoron, was coined to describe Beijing's new development thinking of and approach to reducing its population and relocating certain urban functions in the context of coordinated development of the Beijing–Tianjin–Hebei region. Beijing's downsizing seems to be taking effect. From 2015 to 2020, the share of residents in the central city area in the whole city decreased from 59.3 per cent to 50.2 per cent (Li, 2022). The official discourse celebrated this, claiming that Beijing is the first Chinese city that has achieved reduction-based development.

The basis for this celebration is crude. While megacities like Beijing set caps for population and strive to downsize, some smaller cities are struggling with urban shrinkage—the flight of population to larger cities. Urban shrinkage is both celebrated and lamented among Chinese cities, exposing the exacerbated intercity imbalances. Top cities set urban shrinkage as a planning goal and rebrand it as a new development mode, like reduction-based development. Some cities at the bottom of the urban hierarchy are making efforts to prevent it from happening, trying to retain their own populations. These shrinking cities mostly have difficulty in the economic transition from an industrial or resource-based to post-industrial economy.

Beijing's reduction-based development is not as glossy as the government has propagated. It is a battleground of competing interests, creating new problems and new winners and losers. On 18 November 2017, a fire in a migrant settlement in Beijing killed 19 people. Beijing has numerous such settlements; informal and low-quality, they provide necessary shelters for many migrant workers and families seeking a living in the capital. After the fire, the city government launched an aggressive campaign, evicting thousands of so-called 'low-end population' (*di duan ren kou*) out of these settlements and the city in the harsh winter.

Cai Qi, Beijing's then party secretary and a protégé of Xi Jinping, orchestrated this campaign. The government justified this campaign as integral to reduction-based development of the city and coordinated development of the region, both endorsed by Xi. The campaign, its aggressive approach, and the derogatory term 'low-end population' outraged people, but these did not seem to influence the trajectory of Cai Qi's political career. He was elevated into the Politburo Standing Committee—the top power organ of the CPC—in late 2022. In this promotion, Cai Qi's connection with and loyalty to Xi Jinping seemed to count more than his performance in governing the capital city.

On 10 May 2023, Xi Jinping visited Xiong'an. In the subsequent two days, he visited other places in Hebei, convening meetings with local leaders to promote coordinated development of the Beijing–Tianjin–Hebei region. Xi's visit to Xiong'an attracted much attention and surmise. He praised Xiong'an's construction progress in the six years since its launch in 2017 as 'miraculous', and he expressed the importance of maintaining 'confidence' and 'persistence' to achieve its success. This was Xi's third visit to Xiong'an. But this visit was unusual: Xi was accompanied by three CPC Politburo Standing Committee members: Li Qiang, Cai Qi, and Ding Xuexiang. They are all Xi's protégés and were promoted into the top power organ at the 20th CPC National Congress in October 2022, when Xi secured a third term in office and amassed unreserved power. Heading such a high-profile team to visit Xiong'an, Xi reaffirmed his determination to boost the city's progress, which has been debated and doubted. The participation of Li Qiang, in his role as the premier, in this visit aroused interesting observations. In Chinese political tradition, it is uncommon for both top leaders—the president and the premier—to inspect one place outside Beijing together. Having the new premier Li Qiang participate in the visit was a political gesture to show not only that Xiong'an is an important project but that its importance is a consensus among the top leaders. It is interesting to note that the ex-premier, Li Keqiang (in office 2013–2023 and sadly passed away in October 2023), never visited Xiong'an. This was also a political gesture.

The Beijing–Tianjin–Hebei region is being reimagined by a strong political will. Politics has prevailed over other factors in the reshaping of the region to achieve coordinated development. This process has pros and cons, and it involves winners and losers. Top-down directives and government actions can generate some immediate effects, sometimes at the cost of those who cannot have their voices heard. 'Top-level design' often lacks the deliberation, debates, and critical scrutiny that are necessary for ensuring the success of such megaprojects.

Politics can be changing, transient, and unpredictable. Politically-backed projects can be bold, but high-stakes. The coordinated development of a megaregion like the Beijing–Tianjin–Hebei region and the building of a new city like Xiong'an will surely outlive the duration of a politician's will, power, and regime. Chinese people are not unfamiliar with megaprojects that were initiated by a political will but ended up differently.

One-city development for metropolitan circles

Under the new planning system discussed earlier, two national policy documents have been issued specifically concerning the planning for metropolitan circles. In February 2019, the NDRC issued the *Guiding Opinions on Cultivating and Developing Modern Metropolitan Circles*. In September 2021, the MNR issued the *Practical Codes for Territorial Spatial Planning of Metropolitan Circles*. These two documents provide guidance for the making of plans for metropolitan circles from the perspectives of development planning and territorial spatial planning, respectively. The release of these documents also reflects a recognition of the importance of planning for metropolitan circles at the central government level. However, the nature and authority of these documents in the new planning system lack clarity. This impacts the implementation and enforcement of them in practice.

The NDRC's Guiding Opinions identifies these key areas for the development of metropolitan circles:

- Integrating infrastructures and facilities.
- Enhancing intercity industrial division of labour and cooperation.
- Accelerating the development of a unified and open market.
- Facilitating joint provision of and shared access to public services.
- Strengthening co-protection and co-governance of ecosystems.
- Advancing urban-rural integration.
- Establishing an integrated development mechanism.

(NDRC, 2019b)

To enable metropolitan circle development in these areas, the document stresses a need for coordinated planning and proposes:

> Exploring approaches to formulating development plans and special plans in key areas with a central objective of enhancing the development quality and modernisation level of metropolitan circles. Strengthening the organic articulation between metropolitan circle plans, city cluster plans, and municipal master plans to ensure coordination and convergence of them.
>
> (NDRC, 2019b)

These three plan types—metropolitan circle plans, city cluster plans, and municipal master plans— cover three territorial spatial scales: city cluster is the largest and contains metropolitan circles, which further contain member cities. Geospatially, the metropolitan circle plan sits between the city cluster plan and the municipal master plan.

The MNR's Practical Codes specifies the technical aspects of a territorial spatial plan for metropolitan circles, including principles, major contents, process, and presentation. The Practical Codes prioritises principles like co-governance, coordination, deliberation, communication, and sharing between governments horizontally and vertically to reach consensus and collaboration (Ministry of Natural Resources, 2021). These principles capture well the necessity of advocating collaborative planning for metropolitan circles. However, they seem highly repetitive with those principles set in the NDRC's Guiding Opinions. This raises critical questions about the articulation between the development plan and the territorial spatial plan of a metropolitan region.

After the release of these documents, there has been a surge in making metropolitan circle plans, including development plans and territorial spatial plans. By January 2024, the NDRC had approved development plans for ten metropolitan circles: Nanjing, Fuzhou, Chengdu, Changsha–Zhuzhou–Xiangtan, Xi'an, Chongqing, Wuhan, Hangzhou, Shenyang, and Zhengzhou. As for territorial spatial plans, the governments of Shanghai, Zhejiang province, and Jiangsu province have teamed up and made the *Spatial Coordinative Plan for the Greater Shanghai Metropolitan Circle* with agreement and instruction of the MNR. Released to the public in September 2022, this plan is said to be China's first intergovernmental, cross-jurisdictional, and deliberative territorial spatial plan for a megaregion (further discussed in Chapter 4).

'One-city development' (*tong cheng hua fa zhan*) is the central notion in the planning for metropolitan circles. It is essentially about coordinating the development of several cities within a metropolitan circle into a state in which they function and interact like one city. The *14th Five-Year Plan* (2021–2025) contains a section on 'building modernised metropolitan circles', stating:

> Establish on the central cities [of metropolitan circles] that have strong radiating and leading powers, enhance the coordinated development level of the one-hour commuting circles, and cultivate and develop a batch of modernised metropolitan circles with a high degree of one-city development.
> (Chinese Government, 2021, p. 64)

Several cities within a metropolitan circle are geographically and functionally connected but administratively separated (see Chapter 1). As a result, the development of them is often fragmented, uncoordinated, and unbalanced. The imperative of coordinating them into one city in terms of governance, planning, functioning, infrastructure, and public services is challenging but fulfilling. Several metropolitan circles are pioneering such efforts. The Chengdu metropolitan circle is one of them.

Planning the Chengdu metropolitan circle

Chengdu is a well-studied case of China's coordinated urban-rural development, which has been a national policy since 2003. Chengdu, a municipality that has both urban districts and rural surrounds within its administrative border, has pioneered in exploring coordinated development of both urban and rural areas. For their experimentality and success, these practices have been labelled 'the Chengdu model' (Chen et al., 2019; Ye et al., 2013). Now, a similar coordinated development drive is extending across the border of Chengdu city to include its surrounding cities, which together constitute the Chengdu metropolitan circle. This time, it is once again a pioneer in advancing the planning for a metropolitan circle.

In 2020, the Sichuan Provincial Development and Reform Commission organised the making of the *Development Plan for the Chengdu Metropolitan Circle*, with the participation of agencies in member cities—Chengdu, Deyang, Meishan, and Ziyang. These four cities cover a total area of 33,100 km^2 and had a permanent population of 29.66 million at the end of 2020 (Sichuan Government, 2021). On 18 November 2021, the NDRC formally approved the plan. It was the third development plan for a metropolitan circle—after Nanjing and Fuzhou—which was approved by the NDRC after it released the *Guiding Opinions on Cultivating and Developing Modern Metropolitan Circles* (2019).

In its approval notice, the NDRC endorses that the Sichuan government should oversee the plan's implementation—providing guidance, solving problems arising from implementation, undertaking evaluation, and drawing out experiences and lessons. The constituent cities are responsible for the plan's implementation and for co-making special plans and annual progress reports on the achievement of the planning objectives. The approval notice highlights the lead role of Chengdu, as the central city, in achieving 'one-city development' for the metropolitan circle, especially in areas of infrastructure and connectivity, modern industrial collaboration, opening, sharing of public services, and ecological and environmental protection and governance. The prime goal is to build a modern metropolitan circle with national influence and further to boost the construction of the Chengdu–Chongqing Double-City Economic Circle—a major city cluster in southwest China.

This plan sets both specific and unspecific targets for the metropolitan circle development until 2025: an urbanisation rate for permanent population of 75 per cent; total regional GDP of more than RMB 3.3 trillion (an increase of 53 per cent from RMB 2.15 trillion in 2019); a disposable income level for urban and rural residents close to that of the eastern developed regions (Sichuan Government, 2021). It also sets a long-term outlook of becoming a modern metropolitan circle with international competitiveness till 2035 in alignment with the timeline of national development in terms of realising 'basic' modernisation by then (see Chapter 1).

Broadly aligned to the key areas for the development of metropolitan circles identified in the NDRC's *Guiding Opinions on Cultivating and Developing Modern Metropolitan Circles* (2019), this plan for the Chengdu metropolitan circle identifies these major areas for implementation and action:

- Optimising the spatial structure of the metropolitan circle.
- Accelerating connectivity and infrastructure.
- Coordinating and enhancing innovation-led development.
- Co-building high-end industrial clusters.
- Improving opening and cooperation.
- Facilitating public services access and sharing.
- Enabling co-protection and co-governance of ecosystems.
- Reforming governance mechanisms and systems.

(Sichuan Government, 2021)

The plan maps a spatial structure comprising two development axes and three industrial development belts (Figure 2.3). This structure spreads across the four member cities of the Chengdu metropolitan circle and links it with

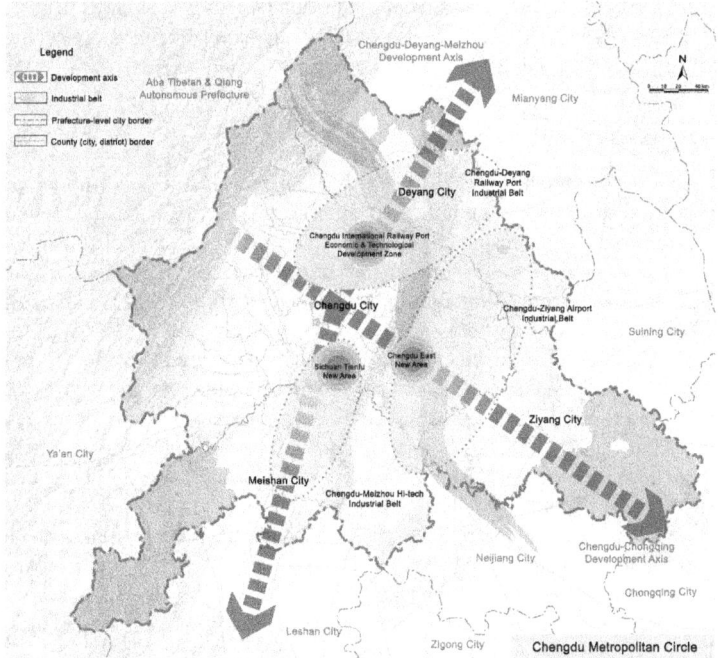

Figure 2.3 Spatial structure for development of the Chengdu metropolitan circle
Source: Sichuan Government (2021), recreated by the author.

the neighbouring Chongqing metropolitan circle. Spatialising the vision of the metropolitan circle, especially the vision of its economic development, this map seems more imaginative than substantive.

The making of the *Development Plan for the Chengdu Metropolitan Circle* is said to have involved deliberations between the four member cities, public participation, and consultations with 20 social stakeholders—people's congress representatives, political consultative delegates, entrepreneurs, and urban and rural residents—in setting goals, agenda, evaluation system, spatial layout, and strategic programs. But it is not clear to what extent this collaborative process has been real or tokenistic.

The Sichuan government established the Leading Group Office for Chengdu–Deyang–Meishan–Ziyang One-City Development, which is called One-City Development Office in short. The party secretaries of the four cities take turns in being the group leader. This office is responsible for the planning of the Chengdu metropolitan circle, vertical articulation and horizontal coordination of the metropolitan circle plan, and its articulation with the making and implementation of other major plans in the four member cities. Compared with similar offices for coordinating the planning and development of metropolitan circles, this office seems active in proposing initiatives, organising activities, and engaging the public.

Articulating regional plans

China's new planning system is triggering and necessitating a new round of making plans of different types and at different levels, as illustrated in Figure 2.1. In late 2022, the making of the *National Territorial Spatial Outline Plan (2021–2035)*—the first such plan at the national level—was completed by the MNR and was released for full implementation starting in 2023. In August 2023, the *Jiangsu Provincial Territorial Spatial Plan (2021–2035)* was approved by the State Council. This is the first territorial spatial plan for a province that has been completed and been approved by the central government. Many plans—either development plans or territorial spatial plans—have been made under the new planning system; more will be made in the future. These seem to suggest the start of a new chapter in the Chinese planning system and a new era of regional planning.

As stated earlier, the regional plan has neither a statutory status nor a corresponding plan level in the new planning system. It is an 'articulator' plan—articulating between plan types and between plan levels. While the new planning system has a central objective of streamlining planning governance, it leaves a grey area for regional planning.

In May 2023, the *Territorial Spatial Plan for the Chengdu–Chongqing Double-City Economic Circle (2021–2035)* was on for public consultation. According to public reportage, this territorial spatial plan for the Chengdu–Chongqing city cluster has been made by governments of the two megacities under the guidance of the MNR. The Chengdu metropolitan circle is part of the Chengdu–Chongqing city cluster. The above 2021 *Development Plan for the Chengdu Metropolitan Circle* is a 'regional plan' under the development planning system (see Figure 2.1). While articulating with upper-level plans for the Chengdu–Chongqing city cluster, it also serves as the basis for making a territorial spatial plan for the metropolitan circle and special plans in various sectors. Within a short timeframe of less than two years, one development plan has been made for the Chengdu development circle, and one territorial spatial plan has been made for the Chengdu–Chongqing city cluster. One important question to ask is how these are going to be articulated—between themselves and with other plans for this megaregion—in plan making, governance, and implementation. This is the materialisation of the grey area for regional planning in the new planning system.

Regional planning—a subsector of China's new planning system—remains unclarified and uncertain in terms of planning status, planning process and standards, and planning governance and implementation. The recent regional plans at various scales are pioneers in testing and advancing Chinese regional planning. Not only do they provide useful experiences and lessons, but they also raise important questions about how to improve the planning and governance of China's megaregions.

References

Chen, C., LeGates, R., & Fang, C. (2019). From coordinated to integrated urban and rural development in China's megacity regions. *Journal of Urban Affairs*, *41*(2), 150–169. https://doi.org/10.1080/07352166.2017.1413285

Chinese Government. (2021). *The People's Republic of China's 14th five-year plan for national economic and social development and outline objectives of the 2035 vision*. [in Chinese]. NDRC. http://www.gov.cn/xinwen/2021-03/13/content_5592681.htm

Hebei Government. (2018, April). *Hebei Xiong'an New Area outline plan*. [in Chinese]. Xinhuanet. http://www.xinhuanet.com/2018-04/21/c_1122720132.htm

Hu, R. (2020). *The Shenzhen phenomenon: From fishing village to global knowledge city*. Routledge. https://doi.org/10.4324/9780367815653

Hu, R. (2023). *Reinventing the Chinese city*. Columbia University Press.

Li, Z. (2022, 24 February). *Beijing takes a substantial step in reduciton-based develpoment and becomes the first Chienseè city of doing so*. [in Chinese]. http://finance.people.com.cn/n1/2022/0224/c1004-32358783.html

Ministry of Natural Resources. (2021). *Practical codes for territorial spatial planning of metropolitan circles*. [in Chinese]. http://gi.mnr.gov.cn/202109/P020210910456249741023.pdf

NDRC. (2019a, 27 November). *Beijing-Tianjin-Hebei coordinated development*. [in Chinese]. https://www.ndrc.gov.cn/gjzl/jjjxtfz/201911/t20191127_1213171_ext.html

NDRC. (2019b). *Guiding opinions on cultivating and developing modern metropolitan circles*. [in Chinese]. www.gov.cn/xinwen/2019-02/21/content_5367465.htm

SCMP Reporter. (2006, 27 February). Beijing's 'poverty belt' raises alarm. *South China Morning Post*. https://www.scmp.com/article/538193/beijings-poverty-belt-raises-alarm

Sichuan Government. (2021). *Development plan for the Chengdu metropolitan circle*. [in Chinese]. https://www.sc.gov.cn/10462/zfwjts/2021/11/29/40678782564141e68f4d1d27180befb9/files/d359ac2bcce440c782b597db912491f2.PDF

Song, Y. (2017). Retrospect and prospect of the coordinated development of Beijing, Tianjin and Hebei. [in Chinese]. *Urban and Environmental Studies*, (2), 3–15.

Ye, Y., LeGates, R., & Qin, B. (2013). Coordinated urban-rural development planning in China: The Chengdu model. *Journal of the American Planning Association*, 79(2), 125–137. https://doi.org/10.1080/01944363.2013.882223

Yeh, A. G.-O., & Chen, Z. (2020). From cities to super mega city regions in China in a new wave of urbanisation and economic transition: Issues and challenges. *Urban Studies*, 57(3), 636–654. https://doi.org/10.1177/0042098019879566

3 Developing metropolitan circles
Issues and challenges

'Broken-head roads' (*duan tou lu*) refer to roads that stop abruptly; 'bottleneck roads' (*ping jing lu*) refer to segments where roads of inconsistent width or numbers of lanes interconnect. These phenomena often happen at the intersections of two cities or administrative units. Used metaphorically, they are often quoted as negative examples of a lack of transport planning coordination between two neighbouring cities. Lack of intercity planning coordination does not just exist in transport; it exists in almost every major area of achieving 'one-city development' for metropolitan circles (see Chapter 2).

From a megaregional perspective, what attribute best describes the relationship between member cities of a metropolitan circle?

One proposition is competition, arguing that these cities compete for opportunities, resources, investment, and talent. This is true since intercity competition is a global urban phenomenon and has been escalating in an increasingly neoliberalised environment. It is also a general belief that intercity competition has contributed to the dynamism and growth of the Chinese economy in the 'reform and opening-up' era. But competition is more a generalised than nuanced description of intercity relationship within a metropolitan circle. The central city dominates and defines a metropolitan circle. The surrounding cities are not competitors of the central city on an equal base in terms of size, economic power, and political status. In a way, these surrounding cities are subordinate to the central city.

But all the cities in a metropolitan circle are administratively independent from each other. They are all prefecture-level cities (PLCs) (*di ji shi*) in the Chinese administrative system, sitting between the higher-level provinces and the lower-level urban districts, counties, or county-level cities (see also Chapter 1). Of course, the central city is of higher status in general perception for its size and importance. The central cities of metropolitan circles are mostly provincial capitals. Some of these provincial capitals are so-called sub-provincial-level cities (*fu sheng ji shi*), reflecting the status of their top leaders who are appointed at this level and are managed directly by the central government (see also Chapter 1). These capital cities are still PLCs. But the appointment of their top leaders at a higher level grants them

36 Developing metropolitan circles

a sort of higher political status and more power than the other PLCs in the administrative hierarchy. Within a metropolitan circle, the surrounding cities simply do not have the capacity, status, and power to compete with the central city.

From a megaregional perspective, fragmentation better captures the intercity relationship within a metropolitan circle than competition. These cities are fragmented from each other in terms of governance and planning, presenting obstacles for achieving integrated, coordinated regional development. The prime imperative for coordinating metropolitan circles is then how to translate the fragmentation into collaboration (see also Chapter 1). This imperative applies to almost every aspect of 'one-city development' of a metropolitan circle (see Chapter 2), which, among other things, includes economic development, connectivity, and investment.

Economic development

Contexts and policies

Collaborative economic development across a metropolitan circle is a growing imperative as well as opportunity for China's national economy and regional economy. Nationally, the Chinese economy has been transitioning to a 'new normal' (*xin chang tai*) in and from the 2010s. This new normal, in practice and in policy agenda, departs from the high growth—often at two-digit annual growth rate of gross domestic product (GDP)—of the Chinese economy from the early 1980s. Rather, it is one of medium or even low growth rate, as has been observed in much of the 2010s (Figure 3.1).

In aspiration, the growth under the new normal is one of constant, stable, and high-quality growth. In the new normal economic discourse, innovation occupies a central position. A focal strategy under the new normal is the 'supply-side structural reform' (*gong ji ce jie gou xing gai ge*), which differentiates

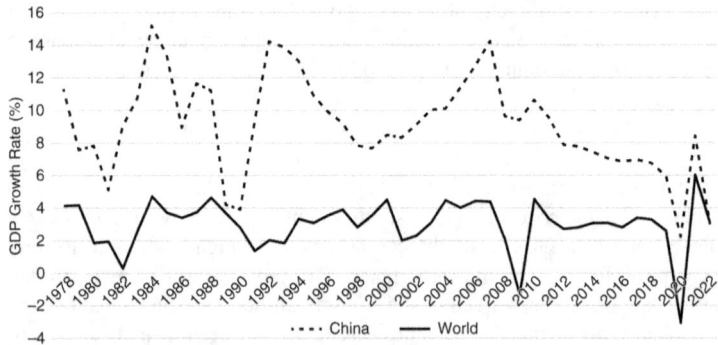

Figure 3.1 Annual GDP growth rates: China versus the world, 1978–2022

Data source: The World Bank (2023), created by the author.

itself from Western supply-side economics and aims at improving productive forces, supply efficiency and quality, and total factor productivity (Xi, 2016). Innovation is expected to play a key role in driving this structural reform. The pursuit of innovation resonates with the exponential advances in digital technology and the rise of the new economy. These new technological and economic factors were captured well by the central government's promotion of 'mass entrepreneurship and innovation' (*da zhong chuang ye, wan zhong chuang xin*) and 'internet plus' (*hu lian wang jia*)—notions advocated by former Premier Li Keqiang (in office 2013–2023)—in transforming and upgrading the Chinese economy.

China is also restructuring its macroeconomic strategy and market, responding to changing international and domestic circumstances. The accelerated globalisation process from the late 20th century seems to be at a crossroads, mixing global economic rebalancing and geopolitics; these have raised justifiable concerns and uncertainties about the prospective post-globalisation (Hu, 2021, pp. 16–21). China is increasingly turning inward to seek new economic growth drivers while still advocating and promoting an integrated global market system that is facing challenges and disruptions now.

The Chinese government is promoting an economic strategy of 'dual circulation' (*shuang xun huan*)—domestic and international circulation— and endorsing the building of a unified domestic market as the primary economic system for a new development pattern. This strategy suggests a need to break through administrative barriers and associated geospatial constraints—which also exist within a metropolitan circle and between metropolitan circles—to enable domestic circulation and to connect with international circulation.

These macroeconomic contexts and discourses contextualise the drive for collaborative economic development in a metropolitan circle. They call for retheorising the regional economy, building upon and extending the conventional agglomeration economics to emphasise the importance of relationality and collaborative advantage in facilitating new economic development paradigms. They also call for revisiting the strategic policies influencing the government-market relationality, an enduring political-economic debate in China and the world and the fundamental question in approaching the development of a regional economy.

The government-market relationality has been the focus of China's economic reform since 1978 when the country launched its modernisation agenda of 'reform and opening-up'. Deng Xiaoping advocated a market economy, explicitly and firmly, since then. But it was not until 1992 that the 'socialist market economy' was enshrined into the orthodoxy of national development. Two decades later, on 12 November 2013, the *Decision of the Central Committee of the Communist Party of China on Some Major Issues Concerning Comprehensively Deepening the Reform* was adopted at the Third Plenary Session of the 18th Central Committee of the Communist Party of China (CPC). It states:

> We must deepen economic system reform by centering on the decisive role of the market in allocating resources, adhere to and improve the basic economic system, accelerate the improvement of the modern market system, macro-control system and open economic system.
>
> (Chinese Government, 2014b)

It has been a long journey to legitimise the market economy in Chinese orthodoxy; it could be an even longer journey to truly fulfil it in economic development. The enduring issue of government-market relationality in China's economic reform applies to economic development for metropolitan circles.

In alignment with the pursuit of market-oriented economic reform, the National Development and Reform Commission's (NDRC) *Guiding Opinions on Cultivating and Developing Modern Metropolitan Circles* sets a principle of 'adhering to the leading of the market and the guiding of the government' and acknowledges the development of metropolitan circles as a 'natural' process (NDRC, 2019).

The Guiding Opinions indicates a need to strengthen an industrial division of labour between member cities of a metropolitan region, achieving urban functional complementarity, enhancing the development of high-end industries in the central city, and strengthening the foundation for manufacturing in medium and small cities. To accommodate the desired industrial division of labour and functional complementarity between member cities, the document stresses differentiated spatial patterns and local characteristics in strategy and planning for economic development in a metropolitan circle.

The *14th Five-Year Plan* (2021–2025) attaches great importance to innovation in building modern metropolitan circles, stipulating collaborative business parks and research and development (R&D) platforms, and the universal circulation and reimbursement of 'sci-tech innovation vouchers'—government-sponsored innovation services and products for supporting small and medium high-tech enterprises—across a metropolitan circle (Chinese Government, 2021b).

Upon and beyond agglomeration economics

The agglomeration economics is still valid in explaining and understanding a regional economy. But it is insufficient to capture the fluidity and elusiveness of the new economy, which is multi-scalar and networked, and which is also concurrently spatialised and non-spatialised. Both the 'space of places' and the 'space of flows' in a 'network society'—using Manuel Castells's (2000) terms—apply to the spatiality of the new economy. These spatial attributes challenge the notion that a metropolitan circle is a spatial scale for economic policy and planning intervention. They further challenge a 'silo' notion that a metropolitan circle can be a spatially-based economic system that not only contains a sort of internal division of labour but also possibly forges a value chain and enables internal collaboration.

These economic notions established upon the spatiality of a metropolitan circle are not wrong; however, they are problematic in capturing the new economic dynamics and their spatial representations inside and outside a metropolitan circle. For example, the Yangtze River delta region—as a city cluster—contains several metropolitan circles (further discussed in Chapter 4). Although these metropolitan circles can be geospatially delineated in an indicative manner, the economic systems between them and within each of them are not as distinct as the spatial delineation indicates. They involve very complicated interwoven economic networks traversing physical and virtual spaces.

In the West and since World War II, there have been three broad stages or paradigms of economic development that focus on comparative advantage, competitive advantage, and collaborative advantage, respectively (Stimson et al., 2006). China has rapidly experienced all these since the early 1980s. Under the paradigm of comparative advantage, the economic development approach has focused on providing more favourable costs for factors of production (land, labour, materials, energy, infrastructure, and tax incentives) than competitors. The paradigm of competitive advantage has emphasised the value factors of efficiency, performance, quality of life, and human and social capital in enabling economic development.

The paradigm of collaborative advantage has now taken hold in economic development for several reasons unique to contemporary contexts. Heightened competition from globalisation, coupled with challenges of environmental sustainability and social equity—all wicked problems—have necessitated more emphasis on collaboration. A growing realisation of these problems, which are persistent and difficult to fix and require efforts that are not possible for individual agents or agencies, has enabled broader international collaboration.

In economic development, the primacy of collaborative advantage is largely attributed to the rise of the knowledge economy and the ascendance of innovation as the most valuable factor of production (Blakely & Hu, 2019). In business, globalised production and retail activities demand a higher degree of coordination and management capacity, requiring collaboration between a diversity of specialised service providers and further contributing to the growth of the knowledge economy and the demand for innovation. Through alliances, partnerships, and other forms of collaboration, competitors fare better and are more likely to achieve a win-win situation. This paradigm of collaborative advantage underpins the logic and the necessity of collaborative economic development both inside and outside a metropolitan circle.

Hangzhou metropolitan circle

The *Development Plan for the Yangtze River Delta City Cluster* (2016)—a national development strategy for the megaregion—sets these directions of 'one-city development' for the Hangzhou metropolitan circle:

- Utilise the region's advantages in entrepreneurship and innovation to incubate and develop new business models and new economic engines like the digital economy.
- Speed up the construction of a national indigenous innovation demonstration zone and an international e-commence comprehensive experiment zone in Hangzhou and a national eco-civilisation pilot demonstration zone in Huzhou.
- Build a pilot demonstration zone for national economic transformation, upgrading, reform, and innovation.

(NDRC & MHURD, 2016, p. 19)

These directions for regional economic development are established upon the competitive advantages of the central city Hangzhou and aim to translate them into regional collaborative advantages in the Hangzhou metropolitan circle and further in the Yangtze River delta region through collaborating with other metropolitan circles (further discussed in Chapter 4). These competitive advantages of Hangzhou's economy are appropriately captured. Within the Chinese economy, Hangzhou is an established leader in the digital economy and its associated industrial sectors. This economic leadership, or competitiveness, has been strengthened in the recent decade (see Figure 3.2).

In history, Hangzhou and its surrounds have been a wealthy region. China's marketisation, the global integration of the Chinese economy, the rise of the new economy, and digital technology have all enabled the growth of Hangzhou into a new economic pole of national leadership and international outreach. Local business culture and entrepreneurship have played an indispensable role in pioneering and advancing its economic transformation. It should be noted that the genesis and trajectory of the economic transformation were unplanned. It was rooted in the DNA of local entrepreneurship and innovation, and has been incubated and spawned in the market. In a 2021 report by the Intelligence Unit of *The Economist*, Hangzhou ranked the first among Chinese cities in terms of growth potential, easing out top-tier cities Shenzhen, Guangzhou, and Shanghai to the second, third, and fourth positions, respectively (The Economist Intelligence Unit, 2021).

Development zones have been an important form of Chinese urbanisation from the early 1990s. Nearly every Chinese city has some form of development zones, but they have fared with mixed outcomes. Recently, there has been a surge of collaborative development zones within metropolitan circles,

Developing metropolitan circles 41

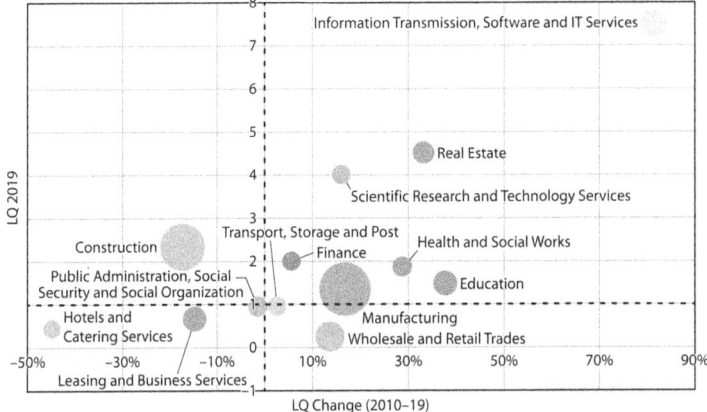

Figure 3.2 Hangzhou's economic base in the Chinese economy, 2010–2019

Notes: The location quotient (LQ) technique is used to measure the concentration of employment by industry in Hangzhou in reference to the national economy. The Y-axis illustrates the LQ in 2019: an LQ value of more than or equal to 1 shows a level of industrial concentration that is higher than or the same as the national average, thus contributing to the local economic base; an LQ value of less than 1 means no concentration of that industry in the local economy in comparison with the national economy, so it does not contribute to the local economic base. The X-axis indicates the LQ change from 2010 to 2019, measuring the time-series trend—strengthening or weakening—of an industry's level of concentration in the local economy. The bubbles represent all the industries that accounted for an employment share of more than 3 per cent—showing a reasonable size and importance of that industry—in Hangzhou's economy in 2019; the bubble size is proportional to the industry's employment share in 2019.

Data source: Hangzhou Government (2022) and National Bureau of Statistics (2022), created by the author.

mostly involving intergovernmental collaboration. In the Hangzhou metropolitan circle, there are a dozen such collaborative development zones. The majority of them are in early stages of planning or development. A salient feature of these development zones is that they are mostly being planned and developed on the fringe of Hangzhou to capitalise on its industrial and innovation spill-overs. The governments of the surrounding cities—Huzhou, Jiaxing, and Shaoxing—have strong incentives for accessing these collaborative economic development opportunities.

Balancing the government-market relationality in the regional economy

An understanding of the Chinese economy needs to be grounded in China's circumstances and its cultural and historical traditions. Among many things, China's economic growth is a result of the combination of the entrepreneurship, exploration, hard work, and risk-taking of the people and the learning and developmental government in developing a socialist market economy. This formula, which has characterised China's 'reform and opening-up' from the late 20th century, has been changing in the recent decade. The recentralisation of governance and political power and a belief in 'top-level design' are restructuring the macroenvironment for economic activities that were previously market based.

The government-market relationality continues to lie beneath many problems and dilemmas identified for regional economic development. Several relational dualities in economic development—government versus market, planning versus unplanning, and top-down planning versus bottom-up entrepreneurship—need to be well appreciated and handled. There needs to be sufficient will and capacity of local governments to recognise the market's role and to engage with the market's actors—entrepreneurs and enterprises—into collaborative and innovative economic development.

The plans for business parks in metropolitan circles are mostly government-led intuitive imaginings. They require rigorous research, evidence-based policy making, good understanding of the innovation-led economic transformation and, most importantly, active participation of the business sectors and the general community. Technically, there is a need for platforms of high-quality economic data collection and dissemination, which are shared across member cities within a metropolitan circle and are open to the public.

The comprehension of and policy response to a regional economy are lagging behind the dynamics of the new economy and the new domestic and international economic contexts. Metropolitan circles do not lack collaborative economic development zones. However, these zones are highly repetitive in vision, strategy, and planning, and their implementation often falls short of their expectations. Many of them are reminiscent of the mushrooming development zones in the 1990s, although they wear the 21st-century hats of 'innovation' and 'collaboration'.

A focus on the formal economy seems to marginalise the booming informal economy in the envisioning of the regional economy. The informal economy is small and obscure individually, but as a whole it is no less important than the formal economy. The informal economy is flexible, innovative, and spontaneous, and has grown out of grassroots ingenuity. It has underlain many aspects of China's economic transformation and is injecting new dynamics into its urbanisation and urban-rural integration in the recent decade. A good example is the exponential growth of 'Taobao villages'—the villages that have a critical mass of e-commerce activities through the platform Taobao—in both urban and rural China, which are supported by the platform economy that is based in Hangzhou and have national and global outreach.

Collaborative economic development in a metropolitan circle should involve, first, collaboration between enterprises, then between the government and the market, and lastly between governments. Intergovernmental collaboration should be centred upon enabling collaboration of the market actors. The boundary between the government and the market should be clearly clarified and demarcated to genuinely fulfil 'capable government' and 'effective market'—notions frequently quoted in the official discourse about government-market relationality—and to prioritise the role of entrepreneurs and enterprises, the market actors, in advancing collaborative economic development. The government needs to understand the limitation of economic planning and strike a balance between 'planning' and 'unplanning' in incubating innovation-led economic transformation.

The government has an imperative for capacity-building to enable collaborative economic development in metropolitan circles, through advancing economic thinking about national and global economic transformations and about the new policy contexts at home and overseas. Such thinking needs to include a deepened understanding of metropolitan circles as a spatial scale for value chains and industrial division of labour in a multi-scalar, networked new economy.

Enabling economic development in a metropolitan circle is not a linear but cyclical, helical process that involves both planning-led development and more often development-pushed planning. It is very important to develop a 'learning government' approach that is responsive, adaptive, and agile in an economic environment of increasing change and uncertainty. The government could develop regionwide and even nationwide economic data collection and sharing, and make bespoke economic policies and programs that are based on analysis of evidence and data, rather than on intuition and aspiration.

In planning and designing a collaborative development zone, the art of placemaking will work better than developing a business park or zone by land use and zoning. The conversion of a 'zone' for development into a 'city' for urbanity and the fusion of industries and the city are of crucial importance in incubating innovation, largely through attracting and retaining the creative class and knowledge workers of the new economy.

Connectivity

Contexts and policies

The Chinese definition of a metropolitan circle is based on the one-hour commuting area surrounding a central city (see Chapter 1). Thus, transport infrastructure plays a foundational role in the definition and function of a metropolitan circle. Metropolitan circle transport is integral to China's strategy of becoming 'a strong power in transport' (Chinese Government, 2019a). In recent decades, China has probably been the world champion in transport infrastructure construction, investment, and technology. However, its 'soft power' of transport governance, planning, and management is lagging behind its 'hard power' of building physical infrastructure. Within metropolitan circles, the soft power of collaborative transport governance is hindering the hard power of regional transport.

Regional connectivity is more than transport as an infrastructure, although it is the most important factor of connectivity. It involves multiple dimensions of human mobility, movement of products and services, flow of information and data, and diffusion of knowledge and innovation. Among them, human mobility occupies a central position, responding to the definition of a metropolitan circle based on the one-hour commuting area.

Here, it is important to conceptually differentiate between 'transport' and 'transit'. Regional connectivity is generally perceived, mistakenly, as a matter of transport; it is, in fact, about transit. These two terms have a common etymology, but they have different connotations in appreciating regional connectivity: transport focuses on infrastructure, engineering, tool, and the movement of products and/or people from one location to another; transit focuses on human mobility, transfer, and accessibility. Regional connectivity is centred on human transit, human mobility, human accessibility, human activities, and socioeconomic and environmental implications of these.

Several national policy documents have been released in recent years, setting visions for transport planning and development, with the central one of shifting China from a 'big power' to a 'strong power' in transport. They all have relevance to metropolitan circle transport.

In 2019, the Chinese government released the *Outline Plan for Building a Strong Power in Transport*. Among many things, this outline plan sets an ambitious 'one–two–three' goal: by 2035, China will achieve a transport system of one-hour commute in metropolitan circles, two-hour accessibility in city clusters, and three-hour coverage of major cities across the country (Chinese Government, 2019a).

In 2021, the Chinese government further released the *National Outline Plan for a Comprehensive and Integrative Transport Network*. This document specifies 'door-to-door' one-hour commute within a metropolitan circle via an integrated transport system. The document also sets a goal for nationwide transport: by 2035, China will complete the construction of a comprehensive integrated transport network that is accessible, efficient, green, smart, and safe; and this network will be multi-layered and will enable regional coordination and national and international connections (Chinese Government, 2021a).

Both documents set the year 2035 as a benchmark timeline for achieving their goals, in alignment with the national development goal of achieving 'basic' modernisation by then (see Chapter 1).

The NDRC's *Guiding Opinions on Cultivating and Developing Modern Metropolitan Circles* (2019) specifies 'opinions' on infrastructure planning and delivery to enable connectivity in metropolitan circles. These include a smooth and efficient road network, a rail-based commute in metropolitan circles, an efficient and optimised logistic system, and an integrated civic services and information system (NDRC, 2019). Regional connectivity in these areas involves both infrastructure construction and service provision to support 'one-city development' for metropolitan circles.

The *14th Five-Year Plan* (2021–2025) basically reaffirms similar notions on building transport for modern metropolitan circles. These include a backbone transport structure of intercity and intracity rails; breaking through 'broken-head roads' and 'bottleneck roads' between cities; connections between urban and suburban transport; 'integration of four rail networks' (*si wang rong he*)—main line rail, intercity rail, suburban rail, and intracity rail (metro); and connectivity of various infrastructures (Chinese Government, 2021b).

'Metropolitan circles on rail' is a central notion in the transport planning policies for metropolitan circles. In 2020, the NDRC and relevant transport and railway agencies co-produced *Opinions on Promoting Accelerated Development of Urban (Suburban) Railways in Metropolitan Circles*. These 'opinions' are mostly directional and generic. But the document stresses that city governments are the responsible actors for developing urban (suburban) railways in a metropolitan circle (Chinese Government, 2020). This issue will be further discussed below with regards to the financing of regional infrastructure.

The national strategies and policies have set grand visions and goals for nationwide transport networks, including for metropolitan circles. The key notion is the 'integration' of transport systems classified by transport modes or delimited by urban/administrative areas. They also appropriately point out the manifested problems in metropolitan circle transport and the need to address them. However, they do not reveal the root causes for these problems and how to fix them from a collaborative regional governance perspective.

Zhengzhou metropolitan circle

The Zhengzhou metropolitan circle anchors the Central Plains city cluster, which is at the geographical centre of China's spatial structure of urbanisation (see Chapter 1). Zhengzhou, given its geographical position, is probably China's most important land transport hub, where both north-south and east-west major railways intersect. This centrality had been established when railways dominated China's transport previously. It has been strengthened in the new national transport structure comprising high-speed rail (HSR), expressways, and airlines.

The transport hub role—mainly in the sense of railway transport—of Zhengzhou has not been translated into enhanced connectivity of the metropolitan circle itself, however. While Zhengzhou is well connected externally, its intraregional connectivity has been problematic in terms of both infrastructure construction and service provision.

The Henan Provincial Development and Reform Commission (HPDRC) released the *Zhengzhou Metropolitan Circle Transport Integrated Development Plan (2020–2035)* in April 2021. This is a forerunner transport plan among metropolitan circles. It was produced after the national strategies for both an integrated transport network and metropolitan circle development were in place, as stated earlier. It captures the strategic visions in both documents and incorporates them into this transport plan for the Zhengzhou metropolitan circle.

The transport plan sets grand visions for 2035: by then, an integrated comprehensive transport system—characterised by integrated transport infrastructure, 'one-city' transport services, and modernised governance capacity—will be completed for the Zhengzhou metropolitan circle (HPDRC, 2021). While the plan ticks the right boxes in regard to visions and strategic goals of a transport plan for 'one-city development' of a metropolitan circle, it lacks specificity and concreteness about how to achieve them through intercity collaboration.

Two challenges confront transport planning and development for the Zhengzhou metropolitan circle:

The first challenge involves the transport plan's relationship with other types of plans for the region. Before the release of the *Zhengzhou Metropolitan Circle Transport Integrated Development Plan (2020–2035)*, the *Spatial Plan for the Zhengzhou Metropolitan Circle (2018–2035)* was endorsed by the Henan government in 2019. In October 2023, the *Development Plan for the Zhengzhou Metropolitan Circle* was approved and released, following in the footsteps of other metropolitan circles in recent years. Temporally, this presents an issue: the making of both the spatial plan and the transport plan has preceded that of the development plan, which is supposed to be the lead of these plans in the Chinese planning system (see Chapter 2). This creates issues of compatibility and articulation between these plans.

The second challenge concerns the financing of transport infrastructure. The Henan government has formulated plans for the metropolitan circle, like the transport plan, but city governments are the responsible actors for the funding and implementation of the plans and their projects. The financial burden on city governments is high. As the development of the metropolitan circle has just begun, the benefits of constructing the urban (suburban) transport systems are not yet taking effect, which increases the financial burden and risk of investment. In the Chinese administrative structure, local governments have the least financial resources or powers. This vertical intergovernmental gap requires a high level of coordination while the focus of policy has been on horizontal intergovernmental collaboration. Funding problems have affected transport infrastructure of the Zhengzhou metropolitan circle. As with other regions, it has not yet established a unified infrastructure investment and financing mechanism. These financing issues will be further discussed in the 'investment' section later in the chapter.

From transport to transit

The central problem of connectivity in a metropolitan circle concerns intergovernmental collaboration in regional transport network and intermodal human transit. Intergovernmental fragmentation exists both vertically and horizontally. Vertically, the planning authority for metropolitan circle transport rests with the provincial government; financing and implementation rest with city and local governments. Horizontally, the central city does not always have the administrative authority to engage surrounding cities in regionwide dialogue and action; intercity coordination lacks initiative or drive unless the provincial government takes the lead.

Regional transport planning practices lag way behind the goals set in the national strategies for establishing a comprehensive integrated transport system. While grand visions can be mapped out by higher-level governments, the implementation of them lacks resources, capacity, and funding at city-level governments; and further lacks financing channels and innovative financing approaches that involve private investment.

Many observed problems in China's regional connectivity are not technical transport issues, like how the transport infrastructure should be planned or constructed. They are governance issues—intergovernmental fragmentation, lack of coordination and participation of stakeholders, or lack of regional governance capacity—that are manifested in poor transport delivery and connection. It is very important for decision makers and planners—at both provincial and city levels—to employ systems thinking to approach regional connectivity that is beyond transport. Regional connectivity hinges on the interface between human transit and urban development.

An engineering-minded transport planning approach often fails to capture the complexity of human transit and its social, economic, and environmental implications. Integrated transport planning and provision involves the integration of multiple transport systems and transport modes; more importantly, it involves integration of multiple urban disciplines—humanities, economics, sociology, environmental sciences, and public administration.

Despite top-down endorsement and bottom-up passion, smart transport technology in China does not seem to translate into smart service and management to an extent it should. Public transport is a prime area for utilising smart technology. China's leadership in both digital technology and infrastructure technology—the hard power—needs to be matched by the soft power of governance, planning, and management to enhance public transit services.

Overreliance on public funding or fiscal allocation is not sustainable for long-term strategic infrastructure investment. There are established innovative financing approaches that can help bring in capital and, more importantly, the capacity for infrastructure management and operation from the private sector.

Transit-oriented development (TOD) is more than a property development approach. It is a holistic way of urban thinking about smart growth, integrating aspirations for transit and accessibility, compact and mixed-use development, place-based innovation, the creative economy, smart financing, environmental sustainability, and social equity and inclusion. While not every aspiration in a TOD project can be achieved, the concept puts 'transit' at the centre of urban development—it is an urban philosophy as well as an urban development approach. It is the opposite to many DOT (development-oriented transit—develop first, and plan and construct transport after traffic problems arise) projects that claim to be TOD.

Both human transit and TOD are key concepts in understanding regional connectivity. They are human-centred. And they are integrative of 'transit' and 'development', which are often separated in regional transport planning and development, however.

Investment

Contexts and policies

From a governance perspective, investment marches on finance. The *Communiqué of the Third Plenary Session of the 18th Central Committee of the CPC* in 2013 acknowledged that 'finance is the foundation and an important pillar of state governance' (Chinese Government, 2014a). Similarly, finance is also the foundation and an important pillar of regional governance. However, regional finance confronts fundamental institutional barriers and operational problems, impacting a city government's power, capacity, and political will to invest in projects of regional importance.

China's national policies on investing in metropolitan circles are limited, generic, implicit, or ambiguous.

The NDRC's *Guiding Opinions on Cultivating and Developing Modern Metropolitan Circles* (2019) offers no 'opinions' exclusively on investment. It sets a 'collaborative' principle for investment in coordinated development for a metropolitan circle. For economic development, the document 'encourages' the establishment of a mechanism of industrial cooperation within a metropolitan circle through 'collaborative investment attraction, co-development, and sharing of benefits and taxes' (NDRC, 2019). It stresses the principle of 'co-construction and co-access' in public services between city governments within a metropolitan circle, like in areas of education, health, and aged care, and public facilities of museums, theatres, and stadiums (NDRC, 2019).

For investment in a metropolitan circle, the central notion in public discussions is about developing a governance approach and mechanism to engage both governmental and nongovernmental stakeholders (or 'investors') into 'co-investment' in projects of regional importance and into sharing the costs and benefits of these investment projects.

The co-investment approach and the principle of 'sharing costs and benefits' underpin the technicalities of expanding and securing funding sources and bases in a metropolitan circle, and of the management of an investment project to ensure its return and success. No explicit policies or government documents stipulate how to implement this approach and principle to achieve the desired outcomes. At an operational level, the implementation of them is mainly up to the interpretation, political will, and capacity of the actors—city governments—in a metropolitan circle and the coordination of the higher-level provincial government.

There is no such thing as regional finance in the Chinese fiscal system—which is structured on the administrative hierarchy—in terms of taxing revenues, budgets, and investment planning.

Since the 1990s, China's fiscal system reform has followed a trajectory of growing the central government's financial revenues and financial powers, despite some rebalancing with local governments—the provincial and lower-level governments—in the recent decade. China has implemented a tax-sharing system since 1 January 1994. This system associates administrative powers with fiscal powers and clarifies the ratio of the tax revenues and the types of tax collected between the central government and local governments. Within a province, the sharing of tax revenues between tiers of government—for example, between province and PLCs—is largely determined by the provincial government. Therefore, provincial tax-sharing and fiscal systems differ by province.

Intergovernmental imbalances exist, vertically and horizontally, in the Chinese fiscal system in terms of financial powers, financial responsibilities, and financial capacities. Both the vertical and horizontal imbalances impact a city government's financial resources and political motivation to invest in a metropolitan circle.

Vertically, a structural imbalance of financial powers and financial responsibilities exists between the central government and local governments (provincial and city governments). This vertical intergovernmental imbalance is conceptually illustrated in Figure 3.3. It is empirically evidenced in

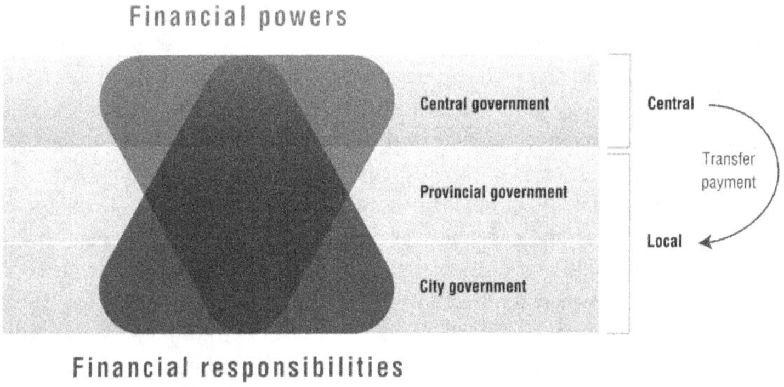

Figure 3.3 Vertical intergovernmental imbalance in financial powers and financial responsibilities

Source: The author.

Table 3.1 Fiscal revenues and fiscal expenditures between the central government and local governments, 2019

	Fiscal revenues (%)	Fiscal expenditures (%)
Central government	46.9	14.7
Local governments	53.1	85.3
Total	100	100

Data source: Liu (2020), created by the author.

Table 3.1. As a result, transfer payment from the central government to local governments is the way to rebalance them. In 2019, of the central government's total fiscal revenues, the central government's own expenditures accounted for 32.1 per cent, and transfer payments to local governments accounted for 67.9 per cent; of the local governments' total expenditures, local fiscal revenues accounted for 63.5 per cent, and transfer payments from the central government accounted for 36.5 per cent (Liu, 2020).

The intergovernmental transfer payment system—from the central government to local governments—mainly includes general transfer payments, special transfer payments, and tax rebates. General transfer payments are at the disposal of local governments; special transfer payments aim to achieve specific development goals of the central government and increase the special appropriations for agriculture, education, health, culture, social security, poverty alleviation, and so on; tax rebates refer to the return of a portion of tax revenues from the central government to local governments after local governments turn over their tax revenues to the central government. In addition to the transfer payments from the central government, provincial governments also earmark special funds for transfer payments to lower-level governments.

China's existing fiscal, taxation, and investment systems and policies are based on administrative divisions from the central down to the local levels of government. Most local governments' revenues do not cover their expenditures. Central government's transfer payments bridge the imbalance between public revenues and expenditures. In the mid-western provinces especially, the central government's transfer payments account for a high proportion (often more than 50 per cent) of their expenditures.

This vertical intergovernmental imbalance often constrains local governments' resources and capacities of and, further, their commitment to investment both inside and outside their jurisdictions. The city governments' financial powers-responsibilities imbalance (more responsibilities than powers) is offset by intergovernmental transfer payments from higher-level governments, a process in which cities compete, not collaborate, by nature. Cities also pursue off-budget financing to support local urban development projects. This has to a great extent triggered the phenomenon of 'land financing' (*tu di cai zheng*)—selling land to increase government revenues—in China's urbanisation (Hu, 2016). Land financing is also incentivising city governments to participate in collaborative development zones within a metropolitan circle. Land financing revenues differ by city and vary by year. In recent years, with the declining real estate industry, shrinking land financing has significantly constrained the revenues of many local governments.

Horizontally, the financial resources and capacities of local governments (both provincial and city governments) differ significantly between regions—eastern coastal regions, central regions, and western regions—across China. The central government's transfer payments play a partial but important role in rebalancing the interregional financial disparities. Unbalanced interregional development is integral to the principal contradiction of national development (see Chapter 1). Within a metropolitan circle, financial imbalance exists among the constituent cities, especially between the central city and its surrounding cities.

Dilemmas and explorations

In China's metropolitan circles, new ways are being explored to improve financing sources and investment approaches in thinking, policy making, and practice. These efforts are still at an initial stage. While challenges and contradictions are explicit, they are pioneers of developing useful experiences and lessons about investing in metropolitan circles.

The *Development Plan for the Yangtze River Delta City Cluster* (2016) has one section exclusively on 'improving a mechanism of sharing costs and benefits'. As discussed earlier, this is an overarching principle set for investing in metropolitan circles in the national policies. This plan document outlines three approaches of investment in the Yangtze River delta city cluster:

- To study the establishment of an investment fund for integrated development of the Yangtze River delta city cluster.
- To establish a mechanism of horizontal interregional compensation for ecological protection.
- To establish an appropriate mechanism for sharing tax revenues and coordinating tax collection.

(NDRC & MHURD, 2016)

These approaches are proposed for the Yangtze River delta city cluster, but they are also applicable to metropolitan circles within the city cluster and elsewhere. While they remain broad and lack specificity, they suggest useful directions along which to explore intergovernmental collaboration and co-investment.

The source of financing is a common—and probably a primary—problem confronting all metropolitan circles. It is for this point that the existing plans are the least explicit, creating uncertainty, ambiguity, and even contradiction in the interpretation and implementation of them.

The newly released *Development Plan for the Chengdu Metropolitan Circle* (2021) describes grand development visions and goals (see Chapter 2), but it has the least clarity about financing:

- To coordinate and innovate investment and financing models.
- To collaborate to bid for relevant government funds and local government bonds to support the key projects of 'one-city development'.
- To explore a development and investment fund to support 'one-city development' with the four member cities as the actors.

(Sichuan Government, 2021)

In financing the many projects included in the *Zhengzhou Metropolitan Circle Transport Integrated Development Plan (2020–2035)*, the document outlines these approaches for implementing or exploring:

- Central government grants, local government revenues, local government bonds, and special loans from development banks.
- Governmental financing platforms, public-private partnership (PPP), TOD, value capture from land sale, tourism development, multiple business models, and commercial developments that involve private capital.
- An investment fund for metropolitan circle transport integrated development.
- A corporation responsible for constructing and operating a cross-jurisdictional transport system.
- A cost-sharing mechanism for investment and operation of transport infrastructure that balances financial responsibilities and financial powers of governments.

(HPDRC, 2021)

In principle, these items capture the core issues of transport integrated development in a metropolitan circle: they are the problems; they are also the areas that require solutions.

Both the above plans for the metropolitan circles of Chengdu and Zhengzhou converge on two notions regarding regional investment:

- First, city governments are identified as the responsible actors for financing and investment.
- Second, explicitly or implicitly, central government funds—via transfer payments—are identified as a possible source of financing.

Both notions represent policy advocacy and aspirations; they both have contradictions inherent in the Chinese fiscal system and the national policy discourse. In the first notion, while city governments are supposed to be the responsible actors for investment in a metropolitan circle, they are the weakest in terms of financial powers and capacities, as discussed above. This contradiction is further related to the second notion that these plans identify higher-level government funds, or transfer payments, as a financing source. This, however, counters the national policy discourse.

The *Reform Plan for the Financial Responsibilities and Expenditure Responsibilities of the Central and Local Governments in Transport Areas* (2019) stipulates the principles in the division of financial responsibilities and expenditure responsibilities between the central and local governments over highways, waterways, railways, civil aviation, postal services, and comprehensive transport. In general, the central government has more responsibilities for special planning, policy decision, supervision, and evaluation, while local governments are more responsible for specific implementation matters such as construction, maintenance, management, and operations (Chinese Government, 2019b).

To interpret this document's implications for investment in metropolitan circle transport: from the central government's perspective, local governments—provincial government or city governments—should be responsible for financing the transport infrastructure in a metropolitan circle. But the document stresses the importance of financial coordination by the provincial government, urging it to take up more financial responsibilities and increase its capacities to support transport as a basic public service, and not to shift too many expenditure responsibilities onto lower-level governments (Chinese Government, 2019b).

In the analysis of the above policy documents at different government levels, there seems a sort of vertical intergovernmental policy 'expectation' in the matter of investment in metropolitan circles:

- The central government 'expects' local governments—provincial and city governments—to commit the investment.
- The provincial government 'expects' city governments to be the major investors and expects the central government fund and support.
- The city governments 'expect' fund and support from higher-level provincial and/or central governments.

These 'expectations' are often translated into vertical intergovernmental 'tension' or 'gaming' in matters of financial responsibilities that are not in balance with financial powers at various levels of governments, as explained earlier.

A vertical intergovernmental tension is mingled with a horizontal intergovernmental fragmentation, creating the prime dilemma for investment in metropolitan circles. Vertical intergovernmental transfer payment remains the de facto mainstream thinking about investment in regional projects— either through national/provincial financial transfer, allocation, or subsidy; or through direct investment. The externality of regional investment, from the perspective of constituent cities, determines that they would expect transfer payment from higher-level governments, or they might fall into an option of taking no action: while collaboration could produce the best outcome, doing nothing would lead to the least bad outcome.

Horizontal intergovernmental investment in a metropolitan circle depends on the establishment of a voluntary, partnership-based co-investment mechanism that functions effectively. Among the tiered fiscal system and relevant laws and regulations, public investment in infrastructure and public services across different jurisdictions is not codified in any statutory document. Rather, it is determined by negotiations among local governments according to the division of financial powers and expenditure responsibilities. It also depends on local governments' financial capacities, which differ significantly between wealthy regions and poor regions. The lack of a practical institutional basis for cross-jurisdictional projects leads to a weak coordination and implementation capacity, which drives up the transactional costs of negotiation, communication, and cooperation among local governments. Coordination by higher-level governments can effectively promote and expedite cross-jurisdictional collaboration.

Intercity co-investment is being explored and advanced in some metropolitan circles. In the Hangzhou metropolitan circle, intergovernmental co-investment in collaborative development zones is a common practice. In the Chengdu metropolitan circle, a 2022 inventory identified 194 major projects for 'one-city development' (Table 3.2). The breakdown of these projects shows the broad areas of investment in the region. These projects amounted to a total investment of RMB 1,224.13 billion, and the annual investment in 2022 was RMB 106.01 billion (Sichuan Government, 2022). Of these projects which are at different stages of development, infrastructure projects have the largest amount of investment—RMB 739.4 billion in total. Industrial development has the largest number of projects (81)—with a total investment of RMB 304 billion—including several collaborative development zones and industrial clusters (Sichuan Government, 2022).

Sub-city level industrial collaboration in the Chengdu metropolitan circle is also worth noting. Jinniu district in Chengdu and Shifang city (a county-level city) in Deyang are developing a collaborative model of 'R&D + manufacturing' to explore a spatially-based division of labour in the unmanned aerial vehicles sector. In this model, R&D is in Jinniu district, capitalising on Chengdu's advantage in talent and high-tech, and manufacturing is in Shifang city, where an industrial park of communications and aerial industries is located. The first project of this model was invested in by Zhonghangzhi, a Beijing-based firm of unmanned helicopters. This firm established its R&D in Jinniu district and its manufacturing in Shifang city; these amounted to a total investment of RMB 5 billion (CMCOCDO, 2022b).

Table 3.2 Major investment projects in the Chengdu metropolitan circle, 2022

Classification	Subclassification	Number of projects
Infrastructure	Transport	63
	Rail (main line, intercity, and urban)	11
	Expressway	12
	Urban axis and thoroughfare	22
	Intercity 'broken-head road'	7
	Tourism transport	3
	Transport hub	8
	Civic facility	9
Subtotal		72
Industrial development	Manufacturing	39
	Modern service	34
	Modern agriculture	8
Subtotal		81
Public service	Education	7
	Health and hospital	7
	Urban governance	1
	Culture and tourism	10
Subtotal		25
Ecological protection	Water resource	8
	Green network	3
	Pollution treatment	5
Subtotal		16
Total		194

Data source: CMCOCDO (2022a), created by the author.

These two sub-city governments are now co-planning the establishment of Jinniu–Shifang Collaborative Park. Based in Shifang Economic and Technological Development Zone, this park aims to advance the model of 'R&D + manufacturing' for collaborative economic development. The collaborative approaches include liaison meetings between government leaders and departments, co-investment in joint companies through state-owned enterprises (SOEs), and the establishment of joint investment-inviting groups (CMCOCDO, 2022b). Similar sub-city government collaboration in economic development is also occurring in the Hangzhou metropolitan circle.

Investment in metropolitan circles involves both vertical and horizontal intergovernmental co-investments. In China, there is a possibility of 'horizontalising' the vertical intergovernmental transfer payment to horizontal intergovernmental co-investment. For example, the national/provincial government can become a co-investor in a project that is of regional importance on an equal basis with city governments—all via the state-owned financing and investment platform companies. These co-investors can further include private investors. This approach can be ensured by an investment governance entity that is endorsed by a higher-level government and participated by constituent local authorities, but the entity remains independent in management and operation.

Further, diversified and innovative financing and investment need to include both governmental and nongovernmental stakeholders and engage them in a mechanism of co-investment and sharing of costs and benefits. It is worth exploring and promoting market-based funding and financing approaches and tools for dedicated regional investment purposes.

References

Blakely, E. J., & Hu, R. (2019). *Crafting innovative places for Australia's knowledge economy*. Palgrave Macmillan. https://doi.org/10.1007/978-981-13-3618-8

Castells, M. (2000). *The rise of the network society* (2nd ed.). Blackwell. https://doi.org/10.1002/9781444319514

Chinese Government. (2014a, 16 January). *Communiqué of the Third Plenary Session of the 18th Central Committee of the CPC*. http://www.china.org.cn/chinese/2014-01/16/content_31213800_2.htm

Chinese Government. (2014b, 16 January). *Decision of the Central Committee of the Communist Party of China on some major issues concerning comprehensively deepening the reform*. http://www.china.org.cn/china/third_plenary_session/2014-01/16/content_31212602.htm

Chinese Government. (2019a). *Outline plan for building a strong power in transport*. [in Chinese]. www.gov.cn/zhengce/2019-09/19/content_5431432.htm

Chinese Government. (2019b). *Reform plan for the financial responsibilities and expenditure responsibilities of the central and local governments in transport areas*. [in Chinese]. www.gov.cn/zhengce/content/2019-07/10/content_5407908.htm?trs=1

Chinese Government. (2020). *Opinions on promoting accelerated development of urban (suburban) railways in metropolitan circles*. [in Chinese]. http://www.gov.cn/zhengce/content/2020-12/17/content_5570364.htm

Chinese Government. (2021a). *National outline plan for comprehensive and integrative transport network*. [in Chinese]. www.gov.cn/gongbao/content/2021/content_5593440.htm

Chinese Government. (2021b). *The People's Republic of China's 14th five-year plan for national economic and social development and outline objectives of the 2035 vision*. [in Chinese]. NDRC. http://www.gov.cn/xinwen/2021-03/13/content_5592681.htm

CMCOCDO (Chengdu Metropolitan Circle One-City Development Office). (2022a, 21 February). *Inventory of major projects in the Chengdu metropolitan circle 2022*. [in Chinese]. http://www.cdmztch.com/city/id/917.html

CMCOCDO. (2022b, 14 April). *R&D + manufacturing Jinshi Collaborative Park construction speeding up*. [in Chinese]. www.cdmztch.com/news/id/1082.html

Hangzhou Government. (2022). *Hangzhou statistical yearbooks*. [in Chinese]. http://www.hangzhou.gov.cn/col/col805867/index.html

HPDRC. (2021). *Zhengzhou metropolitan circle transport integrated development plan (2020–2035)*. [in Chinese]. https://fgw.henan.gov.cn/2021/04-19/2128736.html

Hu, R. (2016). China's land use and urbanization: Challenges for comprehensive reform. In J. Garrick & Y. C. Bennett (Eds.), *China's socialist rule of law reforms under Xi Jinping* (pp. 122–133). Routledge. https://doi.org/10.4324/9781315666129

Hu, R. (2021). *Smart design: Disruption, crisis, and the reshaping of urban spaces.* Routledge. https://doi.org/10.4324/9780367822453

Liu, K. (2020). *Central-local fiscal relationships in China.* [in Chinese]. National People's Congress of China. www.npc.gov.cn/npc/c30834/202008/08bd6bb3168e4916a2da92ac68771386.shtml

National Bureau of Statistics. (2022). *China statistical yearbook.* [in Chinese]. http://www.stats.gov.cn/tjsj/ndsj/

NDRC. (2019). *Guiding opinions on cultivating and developing modern metropolitan circles.* [in Chinese]. www.gov.cn/xinwen/2019-02/21/content_5367465.htm

NDRC & MHURD (Ministry for Housing and Urban-Rural Development). (2016). *Development plan for the Yangtze River delta city cluster.* [in Chinese]. NDRC. https://www.ndrc.gov.cn/xxgk/zcfb/ghwb/201606/t20160603_962187.html?code=&state=123

Sichuan Government. (2021). *Development plan for the Chengdu metropolitan circle.* [in Chinese]. https://www.sc.gov.cn/10462/zfwjts/2021/11/29/40678782564141e68f4d1d27180befb9/files/d359ac2bcce440c782b597db912491f2.PDF

Sichuan Government. (2022, 23 February). *Chengdu metropolitan circle has 194 major projects this year.* [in Chinese]. https://www.sc.gov.cn/10462/10464/10797/2022/2/23/f2c724ff2c0141c7ba6dce325bead5ca.shtml

Stimson, R. J., Stough, R. R., & Roberts, B. H. (2006). *Regional economic development: Analysis and planning strategy* (2nd ed.). Springer. https://doi.org/10.1007/3-540-34829-8

The Economist Intelligence Unit. (2021). *China's emerging city rankings 2021: Unpacking opportunities under the 14th Five-Year Plan.* https://www.eiu.com/n/campaigns/china-emerging-city-rankings-2021/

The World Bank. (2023). *GDP growth (annual %).* https://data.worldbank.org/indicator/NY.GDP.MKTP.KD.ZG

Xi, J. (2016, 18 January). Promote supply-side structural reform. *Qiushi.* http://en.qstheory.cn/2021-07/14/c_642163.htm

4 The dragon's head in spatial imaginary

Integrating Shanghai and the Yangtze River delta region

Flowing 6,300 km from the Tibetan Plateau into the East China Sea, the Yangtze River is often metaphorised as a dragon, the Chinese cultural totem, for its long and winding course. This river's significance is more than cultural; it has nurtured Chinese civilisation in the south, just as the Yellow River has done in the north—both are called Chinese 'mother rivers'.

Naturally, rivers are both the settings and issues for regional planning. For both rivers, the central government has set strategies for environmental and ecological protection and socioeconomic development along them, and elevated these as national strategies. The central government has delineated a 'Yangtze River economic belt', canvassing the entire catchment area. This is probably the largest economic belt of its kind in the world in terms of area and population. It contains ten provinces in addition to Shanghai as a provincial-level municipality, which together account for 21 per cent of China's land, and 40 per cent of both its population and economic output (NDRC, 2016). Planning for this region deserves to be a national strategy.

Great cities grow by rivers. The Yangtze River has grown great cities in history and at present. Just name a few of them: Shanghai, Nanjing, Wuhan, and Chongqing. There are numerous cities—large and small—which have grown by the river or have benefited from sitting in its catchment area. Great city regions also grow by rivers. The cities along the Yangtze River have been merging into city regions of various sizes. There are three city clusters—the Yangtze River delta city cluster, Yangtze River middle reaches city cluster, and Chengdu–Chongqing city cluster—as identified in the megaregional structure for China's urbanisation (see Figure 1.2). The Yangtze River delta is the largest city cluster in China; it is also one of the leading global city regions.

Shanghai is the 'dragon's head'—metaphorically and substantively—for its geographical location at the estuary of the Yangtze River as well as for its strategic importance as a gateway city, not only to the region but also to the country. Shanghai's emergence and rise as a great city provides a microcosm for understanding modern China (Hu & Chen, 2019, pp. 2–6). It was no place—compared with those ancient Chinese cities like Xi'an, Luoyang, and Beijing, and even with its neighbouring cities Suzhou and Hangzhou—before

DOI: 10.4324/9781003108405-4

The dragon's head in spatial imaginary 59

1843, when it was opened as a port city for foreign trade and foreign settlements with extraterritoriality. Shanghai's opening was a forced act under the Treaty of Nanking, a result of the British invasion of China. This was a humiliating but critical episode in Chinese history. It commenced the modern transformation of an ancient civilisation, a process fluctuated with tensions, contests, and to-ing and fro-ing. Still, the process remains one of promises, challenges, and uncertainties at present. But the genesis of Shanghai and the Yangtze River delta as a city region traces back to the year 1843.

In 2006, I led a delegation of Australian planning students and professionals on a study tour to cities in the Yangtze River delta. This tour started from Shanghai, and we visited cities upstream along the Yangtze River, including Suzhou, Wuxi, Changzhou, until Nanjing. The delegates were impressed by each city's scale and speed of growth. Every Chinese city seems to have an exhibition hall that contains a grand model showcasing the city's size and vision of urban development. These were beyond the senses and measures of cities in Australia or outside Asia. The delegates were also impressed by the intercity connections. It took 30–60 minutes' drive to reach the next city on an expressway along the Yangtze River. That was before the age of high-speed trains in China. Today, it takes just a bit more than one hour to commute between Shanghai and Nanjing, 300 km apart, by high-speed trains. The chain of these and other cities forges a most dynamic and interactive city region in the world, raising questions and necessity of regional planning.

There are new planning strategies for the Yangtze River delta at various scales—entire delta region, city cluster, or metropolitan circle. The making of these strategies is either top-down or bottom-up. They respond to the new context of China's urbanisation and megaregionalisation and, more importantly, to the escalating demand for integrated planning and development of the region.

It is necessary to clarify the three spatial scales discussed here. The Yangtze River delta region refers to the three provinces of Jiangsu, Zhejiang, and Anhui and one municipality of Shanghai. The Yangtze River city cluster refers to the agglomeration of interconnected cities across these provinces in addition to Shanghai. Within this city cluster, there are several metropolitan circles. These spatial scales, as illustrated in Figure 4.1, are led by Shanghai as the dragon's head.

Yangtze River delta region: One region, unbalanced development

People in Anhui province may feel unsure whether they are part of the Yangtze River delta region. Anhui is an inland province, considerably upstream from the estuary of the Yangtze River. Zhejiang and Jiangsu provinces and Shanghai are nestled together, geospatially and culturally, forging an entity of themselves. *Jiangzhehu*, the Chinese abbreviation of them, represents an image of more

60 *The dragon's head in spatial imaginary*

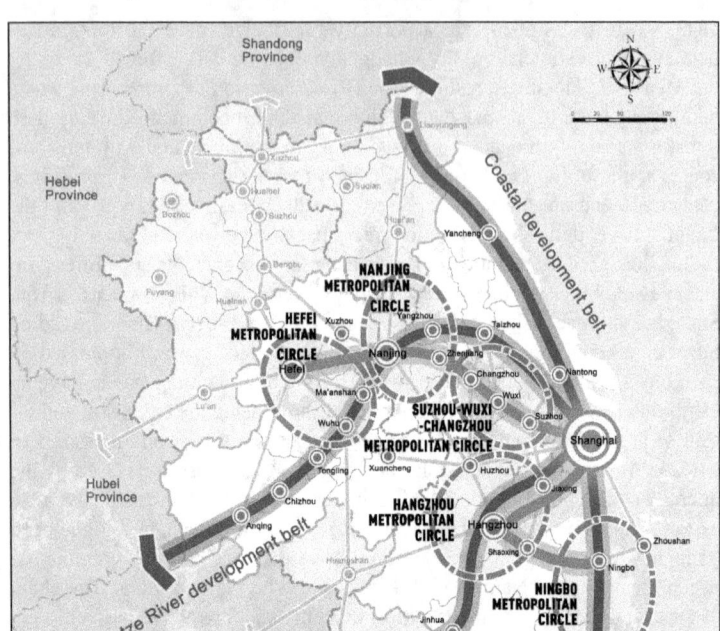

Figure 4.1 Yangtze River delta
Source: NDRC and MHURD (2016), recreated by the author.

advanced development and prosperity in general perception. They are coastal. In history, the area where they merge was more prosperous than elsewhere in China in terms of economy and culture. It is still so today. In modern times, Shanghai has been rising rapidly and now dominates the region.

The delineation of this Yangtze River delta region that contains these three provinces and one municipality is more an administrative construct than an entity of regional development. Considerable intraregional—and intraprovincial—imbalances in socioeconomic development exist. As compared in Table 4.1, Anhui is lagging behind in this region in terms of gross domestic product (GDP) output, economic structure, and residents' income. This is not news. It is typical of the imbalances between coastal and inland

Table 4.1 Major indicators for the three provinces and one municipality in the Yangtze River delta region, 2020

	Shanghai	Jiangsu	Zhejiang	Anhui
Area (km²)	6,341	107,217	105,585	140,140
Permanent population (10,000)	2,488.36	8,477.26	6,468	6,105
GDP (RMB 100 million)	38,700.58	102,718.98	64,613.34	38,680.63
Primary sectors	103.57	4,536.72	2,169.23	3,184.68
Secondary sectors	10,289.47	44,226.43	26,413.95	15,671.69
Tertiary sectors	28,307.54	53,955.83	36,031.16	19,824.26
Residents' disposable income (RMB)	72,232	43,390	52,397	28,103
Permanent urban residents	76,437	53,102	62,699	39,442
Permanent rural residents	34,911	24,198	31,930	16,620

Data source: Shanghai Bureau of Statistics (2021), created by the author.

areas in China, although they are close to each other. Further, there are intraprovincial imbalances in terms of north-south divide. Within both Anhui and Jiangsu provinces, the southern parts are more developed than the northern parts, in history and at present. The Yangtze River is a natural endowment for the comparative prosperity of the southern parts. Shanghai's rise in modern times has enlarged this north-south divide.

But administrative intervention can make a difference to the intraprovincial imbalances. In Anhui province, its capital city Hefei—in the geospatial centre of the province that has a north-south rhombus shape—has been rapidly growing in the recent decade. Hefei's growth has been largely thanks to a whole-province endeavour, policy favouritism, innovation-led economic transformation, and the city government's entrepreneurship and direct involvement in economic decisions and activities (Hu, 2023a, pp. 122–130). The rise of Hefei, as the provincial capital, is rebalancing the north-south divide of development within the province. Several southern cities along or near the Yangtze River, despite their advantageous geospatial locations and historical standing, seem to have been sidelined in the restructuring of provincial development. Anqing, a city along the Yangtze River, was the capital of Anhui in history. Local residents have a strong sense of loss for the city's lacklustre development in the recent decade, especially in comparison with Hefei and other peer cities within the province.

The north-south divide within a province is probably the most prominent in Jiangsu province. The southern part has all the factors for enabling its better development than the northern part: the Yangtze River running through it, the provincial capital of Nanjing along the Yangtze River, proximity to Shanghai, and historical assets of economy, culture, and talent. North Jiangsu and south Jiangsu have contrasting indicators of socioeconomic development and associated images in general perception. This north-south divide is not being narrowed but rather is being enlarged because of the agglomeration effect of the southern cities in the Yangtze River delta.

These intraregional and intraprovincial imbalances justify the imagining and necessity of integrated regional development. On 5 November 2018, Xi Jinping announced that the integrated development of the Yangtze River delta region was elevated into a national strategy at the inaugural China International Import Expo held in Shanghai. Similar national strategies include the Belt and Road Initiative, coordinated development of the Beijing–Tianjin–Hebei region (see Chapter 2), the Yangtze River economic belt (as stated earlier), and the Greater Bay Area (see Chapter 5). A broader context for this inaugural import expo, which has been an annual event since 2018, was the escalating China–US trade war. The Chinese government was attempting to expand its international trade avenues as well as to turn inward to grow the domestic market, responding to the challenges imposed by the trade war. For decades, international trade has been a major driver for the booming Chinese economy. Since the second half of the 2010s, international trade has been increasingly mixed with escalating geopolitics and the Western threat of 'decoupling' or 'derisking'. Integrated regional development fits well with these contexts and aspirations—establishing a connected domestic market and enhancing the global competitiveness of leading regions.

In December 2019, the Chinese government released the *Outline Plan for Integrated Development of the Yangtze River Delta Region*, covering the whole region of three provinces and one municipality. This plan had been anticipated since the integrated development of the region was announced as a national strategy by the top leader one year earlier. What the plan would look like and how it could be implemented raised considerable interest and questions among planners. Before the plan's release, I was in Shanghai and discussed the notion of 'integrated development' of the region with several local planners. They shared a similar puzzle: how the development of a region of such vastness, diversity, and imbalances can be 'integrated' through one blueprint for regional development.

This outline plan is more a manifesto than a plan. It is strategic and general, serving as a guideline for the region's integrated development and subordinate plans for achieving it. For this reason, this outline plan lacks specificity and novelty, but reaffirming many development notions of Xi Jinping's 'new era' in the regional context: a collaborative and innovative industrial system, a connected infrastructure system, co-protection and co-governance of ecology and environment, access to and sharing of public services, collaborative opening, and an innovative mechanism for integrated regional development (Chinese Government, 2019). As commented by local planners, the challenge is how this grand plan is going to be implemented to achieve its strategic vision.

Integrated development is not a new notion for the region. Generally speaking, the less developed area has a stronger aspiration for integration than the more developed area. When I engaged with local planners and stakeholders, I could strongly feel the difference in perception and enthusiasm between Shanghai and Anhui when the issue of integrated development was raised. Contrary to the neutrality and indifference I observed in Shanghai, Anhui demonstrated explicit zeal and action.

In 2008, the Anhui government proposed a regional development concept of 'Wanjiang urban belt'. Wanjiang, a Chinese abbreviation, literally means the Yangtze River segment in Anhui province. The Wanjiang urban belt includes nine cities—either by the Yangtze River or close to it—within the province, which together accounted for 45 per cent of the provincial population and 66 per cent of its GDP in 2008 (NDRC, 2010, p. 1). The Wanjiang urban belt was proposed to accommodate those industries which would be relocated from the Yangtze River delta. The underlying assumption is that those labour-intensive manufacturing industries would move inland, pushed by the coastal area's economic transformation and industrial upgrading. The Wanjiang urban belt has a geospatial advantage of being part of the pan-Yangtze River delta region and will benefit from receiving those industrial relocations.

When I visited Anqing, a city within the Wanjiang urban belt, in 2010, I could tell the local enthusiasm for this regional development concept and its possible opportunity for developing the local economy. I met the president of Anqing Vocational and Technical College, who explained how this concept was shifting the way they would train their students to prepare for the workforce in anticipation of the new development opportunity. Compared with the more developed areas of Jiangsu, Zhejiang, and Shanghai—the core of the Yangtze River delta, Anhui wears a label of 'inferiority' in socioeconomic development. People there have long been keen to drive up the local economy through capitalising on regional spill-overs.

In 2010, the National Development and Reform Commission (NDRC) produced the *Plan for Demonstration Zone of the Wanjiang Urban Belt for Accommodating Industrial Relocations*. This plan proposes a spatial structure of 'one axis, two cores, and two wings' for this urban belt: the one axis includes the chain of six cities along the segment of Yangtze River within Anhui province, including Anqing, Chizhou, Tongling, Chaohu, Wuhu, and Ma'anshan; the two cores refer to Hefei and Wuhu; and the two wings refer to Chuzhou and Xuancheng for their proximity to Jiangsu and Zhejiang provinces, respectively (see Figure 4.2). For each city in this structure, the plan proposes industrial clusters established on both the local economic bases and expected industrial relocations from the more developed neighbouring areas.

This plan demonstrates a clear spatial reductionism in approaching regional economic development. In around 2010, those years after the 2008 global financial crisis, economic restructuring was hotly debated in China: while the coastal and eastern areas confronted an imperative for economic transformation and upgrading, the vast inland and western areas had a prime mission of growing the economy. It was a natural expectation—or wish—that certain industries, especially those labour-intensive manufacturing industries, would move westward.

64 *The dragon's head in spatial imaginary*

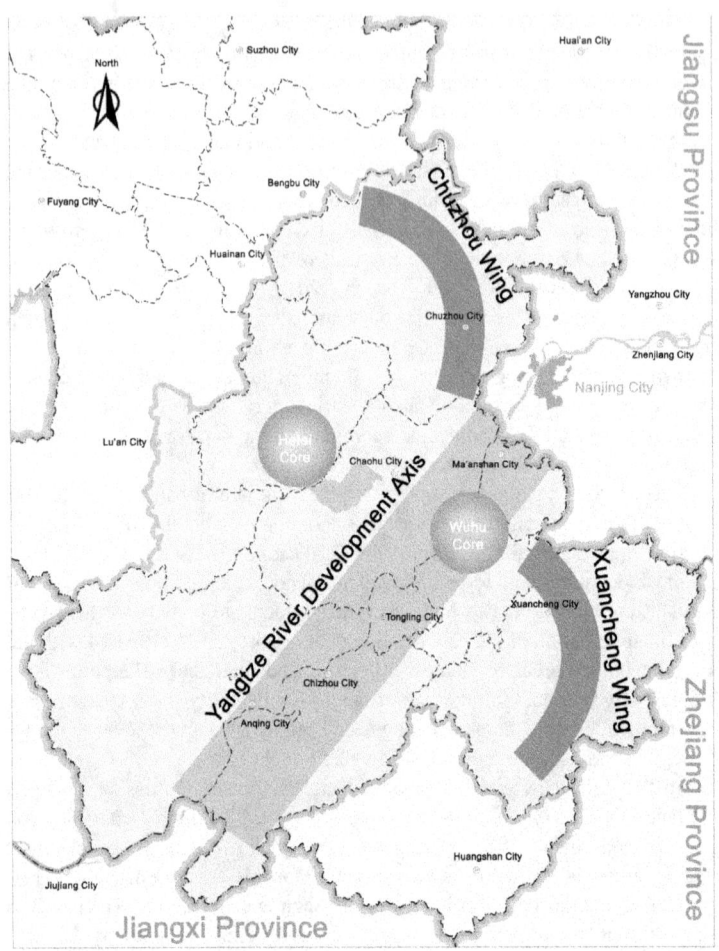

Figure 4.2 Wanjiang urban belt
Source: NDRC (2010), recreated by the author.

The Wanjiang urban belt was imagined in this ethos. However, regional economic development is more complicated and nuanced than this spatial reductionism deduces. It turns out that Hefei has developed the most in the recent decade. Within the Wanjiang urban belt, Hefei is not as advantageously positioned as those cities along the Yangtze River. But it has one—the most important one—advantage that other cities do not have: it is the provincial capital. Hefei's development does not seem to have followed the imagining of accommodating industrial relocations. Instead, it has followed an alternative path of innovation-led development, capitalising on the city's innovation assets and, more importantly, its administrative asset as the provincial capital. Hefei's success in developing a tech cluster to drive the local economy has attracted attention at home and overseas. *The Economist* acclaims a 'Hefei model':

> The city's success owes much to what some call the 'Hefei model'. A unique combination of local government investment and private enterprise, the model has been described as state capitalism at its best.... These so-called strategic, emerging industries now account for over 56 per cent of Hefei's industrial output, compared with less than 27 per cent in 2013.... But Hefei's success suggests that education, industry and geography are not enough. Political incentives must also align.... The Hefei model, on the other hand, requires gumption and daring.
>
> (The Economist, 2023)

However, the imagining of the Wanjiang urban belt has its merits in terms of capturing the spill-overs from the Yangtze River delta. Apart from the exceptional Hefei, the economic development of other cities in the Wanjiang urban belt has varied. Wuhu and Chuzhou have clearly benefited from their proximity to Jiangsu province and, most importantly, to its capital Nanjing. Their GDPs rank second and third in Anhui province now (see Table 4.2). The traditional resource-based cities Ma'anshan and Tongling are facing challenges of not only economic transition but economic growth. Anqing, a strategic major city in history and now, has had a declining economic role in the province and the region. In 2009, its GDP ranked third in the province; in 2021, it ranked fifth (see Table 4.2).

Table 4.2 GDP of major cities in the Wanjiang urban belt (in RMB 100 million), 2009–2021

	2009		2021		2009–2021
	GDP	GDP share (%)	GDP	GDP share (%)	GDP change (%)
Hefei	1,664.84	18.76	11,412.8	26.57	585.52
Wuhu	749.65	8.45	4,302.63	10.02	473.95
Ma'anshan	636.3	7.17	2,439.33	5.68	283.36
Anqing	704.72	7.94	2,656.88	6.18	277.01
Xuancheng	411.61	4.64	1,833.92	4.27	345.55
Chuzhou	479.33	5.4	3,362.11	7.83	601.42
Tongling	325.31	3.67	1,165.58	2.71	258.3
Chizhou	192.4	2.17	1,004.18	2.34	421.92
Anhui Province	8,874.17	100	42,959.18	100	384.09

Data source: Wikipedia (2023), created by the author.

66 *The dragon's head in spatial imaginary*

The interprovincial spill-overs have affected metropolitan circle planning in the region. The geographical location of Nanjing, the capital of Jiangsu province, is interesting: it is closer to Anhui than to most area of Jiangsu. Its functions and influences spill over into Anhui; as a result, the Nanjing metropolitan circle is transverse across both provinces. People in Ma'anshan feel that they are in Greater Nanjing although administratively they are in Anhui province. The *Development Plan for the Nanjing Metropolitan Circle*, which was released in April 2021, formally includes four cities in Anhui—Wuhu, Ma'anshan, Chuzhou, and Xuancheng—in the planning area of the metropolitan circle. Similarly, the Hangzhou metropolitan circle also includes Huangshan in Anhui province in imagining and planning the circle's development. This regionalisation of urban development across provinces complicates as well as demands integrated regional planning and development.

Yangtze River delta city cluster: One city cluster, interlinking metropolitan circles

The Yangtze River delta region, an administrative construct as stated earlier, is anchored by its city cluster. Of the region's total area of 358,000 km^2, the major cities that constitute the city cluster occupy 225,000 km^2, accounting for 63 per cent of this area (Chinese Government, 2019). In the national context, this city cluster accounted for 2.2 per cent of land, 18.5 per cent of GDP, and 11 per cent of population as of 2014 (NDRC & MHURD, 2016). This is a backbone megaregion for national development.

Among the top ten Chinese cities in terms of GDP in 2022, four are located in this city cluster: Shanghai (no. 1), Suzhou (no. 6), Hangzhou (no. 9), and Nanjing (no. 10) (Sohu, 2023). Other leading cities for GDP in the region include Ningbo (no. 12), Wuxi (no. 14), Hefei (no. 21), and Changzhou (no. 25). Proximity to Shanghai and the coast seems to be a major factor for these cities' economic performance. The GDP of Suzhou, a prefecture-level city (PLC) (see Chapters 1 and 3 for PLCs) in Jiangsu province but very close to Shanghai, is more than that of the provincial capital Nanjing. Similarly, the GDP of other PLCs like Ningbo and Wuxi is more than that of Hefei, the capital of Anhui province. These measures attest to the role of Shanghai as the dragon's head in the region and the imbalances between coastal and inland cities.

Geospatially, major cities in this city cluster are more than those located beside or close to the Yangtze River; they extend to Hangzhou Bay, the natural endowment that has nurtured Hangzhou and Ningbo in addition to other cities of smaller sizes. The regionalisation of these cities has forged an interlinked urban region and urban system. But this interlinking also challenges the identification of metropolitan circles—as a distinct urban scale—in this region. This problem will be further discussed below.

In 2016, the central government, via the NDRC and the then Ministry for Housing and Urban-Rural Development (MHURD), released the *Development*

Plan for the Yangtze River Delta City Cluster. This plan compares this city cluster with international counterpart regions in the US, Europe, and Japan in terms of GDP per capita and GDP per km^2. It concludes that the region's development quality was not high, and its international competitiveness is not strong enough (NDRC & MHURD, 2016). The plan also points out that Shanghai's competitiveness as a global city—especially in comparison with New York, Tokyo, and London—is comparatively weak. These global comparisons, together with other imperatives like urban citizenisation of rural migrants, regulation of urban construction and efficient land use, and ecological and environmental protection, call for integrated development of the region, so the plan argues.

The development plan outlines a spatial structure of the region's urban and strategic development (Figure 4.1). This is a spatial imaginary partly based upon existing urban and natural patterns and partly based upon aspirations. This structure contains five metropolitan circles centred around Hangzhou, Ningbo, Nanjing, Hefei, and Suzhou–Wuxi–Changzhou, while Shanghai is the core of the whole city cluster. This delineation of metropolitan circles is the most problematic part of the spatial imaginary, considering the definitions of metropolitan circles in the Chinese planning discourse (see Chapter 1) and the region's interlinking urban development.

Ma'anshan and Wuhu are both scoped within the Hefei metropolitan circle; this is an administrative construct since these cities are all within Anhui province. Wuhu is a major city in its own right and its GDP ranks second in the province (see Table 4.2). Ma'anshan is integral to the Nanjing metropolitan circle. It is questionable to include these two cities within the Hefei metropolitan circle. The Suzhou–Wuxi–Changzhou metropolitan circle contains three major cities, each of which is an economic power in both the regional and national contexts. Suzhou is more interlinked with Shanghai than Changzhou. Geospatially, these three cities are next to each other; functionally, none of them is the central city of the metropolitan circle. The interlinking of these centres defies both the definition and the spatial imaginary of metropolitan circles in the Yangtze River delta city cluster.

A regional spatial imaginary also extends to innovation, a buzzword in the discourse for integrated development of the region. Strategically, the Chinese government identifies four national science centres—Beijing, Shanghai, Hefei, and the Greater Bay Area—two of which are in the Yangtze River delta. Shanghai and Hefei are identified as national science centres for their local innovation assets, which have followed different evolutionary trajectories, however. These local innovation assets have underpinned the imagining of regional innovation.

Shanghai has a home-grown cluster of education and research institutes, which are located in Puxi, the west part of the city. Its innovation brand, Zhangjiang, is based in Pudong, to the east of Puxi across the Huangpu river that runs through the city. This brand is new and is an outcome of planning. One of the four development zones for Pudong New Area, a new urban centre developed from 1990, Zhangjiang specialised in high-tech sectors. Since then, Zhangjiang has expanded both spatially and conceptually. The original Zhangjiang high-tech zone had a planned area of 2 km^2 in 1992 (Hu & Chen, 2019, p. 187). In 2021, the Shanghai government planned an area of 220 km^2 for the Zhangjiang Science City (Shanghai Government, 2021), which has incrementally evolved from the original high-tech zone. Zhangjiang is also the umbrella brand for all the innovation districts across metropolitan Shanghai.

Hefei's path to a national science centre is accidental. It is home to the University of Science and Technology of China and a group of research institutes, which were relocated from Beijing in the 1970s out of concerns about possible Soviet attacks on the capital during the period of tense China–Soviet relationship. These education and research institutes, which were deemed as burdensome when they were first relocated to Hefei, have proven to be endogenous assets in the city's innovation-led economic transformation in the recent decade.

Innovation corridors provide a new avenue for imagining innovation clusters in a regional context. Different from conventional innovation clusters that are precinct-based, innovation corridors are linear, often established or imagined along transport lines. The best-known innovation corridor in the world is probably Boston's Route 128, known as 'America's technology highway', which is often compared to Silicon Valley in terms of innovation clusters. A similar innovation corridor is being imagined in the Yangtze River delta—the G60 Innovation Corridor. This was a bottom-up initiative by the local government and was then endorsed by the central government. The initiation and endorsement of it fit well into the discourse of integrated development of the region and the growing importance of innovation in the envisioning of both regional and national development.

G60 is an expressway linking Shanghai with Kunming, the capital of Yunnan province. Its segment in the Yangtze River delta links Shanghai and several cities in Zhejiang province, including Jiaxing, Hangzhou, and Jinhua. The notion of G60 Innovation Corridor was first proposed by the government of Songjiang, a district of Shanghai. It refers to the innovation cluster along the segment of G60 within Songjiang, which has a length of 40 km and around which there are nine innovation districts of various types—actual or planned. This notion was proposed in May 2016. Two years earlier, Xi Jinping had made the directive that Shanghai should become an innovation centre of global influence. Within metropolitan Shanghai, the innovation hub—as a place or a brand—is Zhangjiang, not Songjiang. But the conception, given the timing of its proposal, seemed to strike a chord with the Shanghai government, which incorporated this corridor into its strategy of building Shanghai into a global innovation centre—a political will from the top leader.

Geographically, Songjiang neighbours Zhejiang province, which is also seeking avenues of capitalising on spill-overs from Shanghai. In July 2017, the G60 Innovation Corridor was extended to include the segments in Jiaxing and Hangzhou—two cities along the G60 expressway in Zhejiang

The dragon's head in spatial imaginary 69

province—according to a strategic collaborative agreement signed by the three governments.

But the Songjiang government, a local government in the Chinese administrivia system, had a more ambitious conception for the innovation corridor: it wanted to extend the corridor across the Yangtze River delta. In June 2018, the G60 Innovation Corridor was expanded to include Suzhou, Huzhou, Xuancheng, Wuhu, and Hefei, which are linked by high-speed rail (HSR), in addition to an extension to Jinhua along the G60 expressway. Altogether, the spatial structure of this innovation corridor links nine cities, forming a V shape with Shanghai—via the focal node of Songjiang—as the head (Figure 4.3).

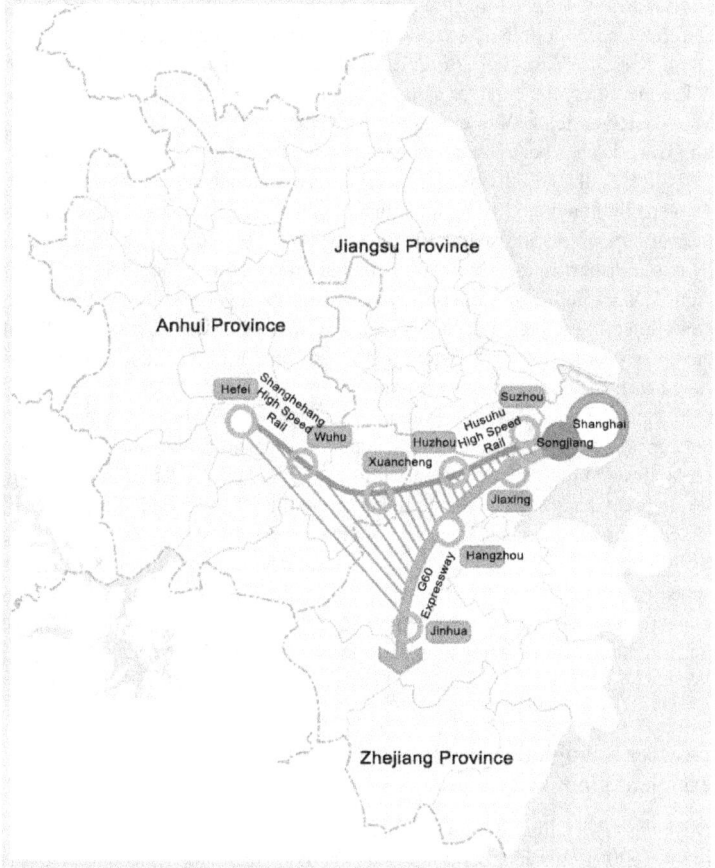

Figure 4.3 G60 Innovation Corridor
Source: Songjiang Government (2022), recreated by the author.

The governments of these nine cities signed a strategic collaborative agreement and announced a Songjiang Manifesto on collaborative construction of the G60 Innovation Corridor to collectively advance innovation-led industrial transformation and to reform innovation ecosystems in the region.

The conception of G60 Innovation Corridor, a regional innovation initiative proposed by a local government, was incorporated into several strategies of the central government. The *Outline Plan for Integrated Development of the Yangtze River Delta Region* released in May 2019 includes this corridor as a pivot for collaborative regional innovation. In November 2020, several central government departments led by the Ministry of Science and Technology co-produced the *Construction Scheme for the G60 Innovation Corridor in the Yangtze River Delta*, aiming to integrate innovation, industrial transformation, and finance into a holistic scheme for the corridor to drive regional development. The *14th Five-Year Plan* (2021–2025), which was released in March 2021, identifies this corridor as integral to the integrated development of the Yangtze River delta. With these policy and planning documents, G60 Innovation Corridor has been incorporated into the national strategy for the region.

However, the G60 Innovation Corridor is more conceptual than substantial. As a spatial imaginary for regional innovation, it has several flaws at the interface of innovation and spatiality. The structure of the corridor is underpinned by two transport lines, which do not link all major innovation nodes in the region. It is an initiative proposed and consistently advocated by the Songjiang government. Songjiang (as part of Shanghai) has been placed, intentionally, at the nodal position of the V-shaped spatial structure of the corridor. However, as stated earlier, Songjiang is not a prime innovation hub of Shanghai. Further, it seems that the several cities—Wuhu, Xuancheng, and Huzhou—are included in the corridor more because of their geographical positions than their innovation capacities. On the contrary, major cities along the Yangtze River like Nanjing, Wuxi, and Changzhou—which are better qualified for becoming members of the corridor—are excluded because of their geographical distance from it. The G60 Innovation Corridor is essentially a local government's advocacy that has appealed to higher-level governments for the notion's selling points of innovation and integrated regional development. It is more a place marketing initiative for Songjiang than an innovation drive for the Yangtze River delta city cluster.

Greater Shanghai metropolitan circle: Striving for the excellent global city region

Dashanghai, a Chinese term that literally means Greater Shanghai, was used in the 1920–1940s. The term's origin cannot be accurately traced. One guess is that it was first proposed by Ding Wenjiang, a Chinese geologist and scholar based in Shanghai then. Ding made great efforts in improving Shanghai's urban management and winning back certain rights of the city's governance from colonial administrations. In 1843–1943, Shanghai was a dual city of a Chinese Shanghai and a foreign Shanghai due to the existence of foreign concessions with extraterritoriality (Hu & Chen, 2019, pp. 2–6). The foreign Shanghai was in the city centre, representing what Shanghai was about at that time—an international city in the Far East, rivalling Paris, London, New York, and Tokyo in terms of economy, architecture, infrastructure, and reputation. In many aspects, the Chinese Shanghai seemed an antithesis of the foreign Shanghai, lacking regulated planning, development, and management.

Dashanghai was a Chinese aspiration for the country's prime city in both geographical and cultural senses. Geographically, the term referred to Shanghai as a region that contained the foreign city centre, which was a humiliating—as well as admirable—existence for the Chinese people and Chinese authorities of various regimes. The term also denoted a cultural pride and an emotional attachment: Shanghai is 'big' and 'great', as *da* literally means.

The term *dashanghai* had great popularity not only in general use but also in urban planning then. It appeared in the title of *Greater Shanghai Plan* (1927–1937). This was China's first modern city plan. Another *Greater Shanghai Plan* was made in 1946–1949. Neither plan was fully completed or implemented due to wars, financial constraints, or regime changes. However, they occupy important positions in Chinese modern planning history: they were the earliest modern urban imaginary in China. After 1949, the term *dashanghai* was no longer in common use in the city's planning. As a cultural concept, it was not in much use, either.

In recent years, a similar notion of Greater Shanghai has been emerging in the regional planning discourse, as it appears in the spatial concept of 'Greater Shanghai metropolitan circle'. This use, however, has significantly different contexts and connotations from those of the 1920–1940s.

In January 2018, the Shanghai government released a master plan for the city—*Shanghai 2035*. This plan 'demonstrates a significant departure from the city's previous master plans in terms of planning thinking, approach, and presentation' (Hu, 2023b, p. 127). This long-term plan sets a strategic vision of 'striving for the excellent global city' (Shanghai Government, 2018). It also delineates a 90-minute commuting circle, which extends outside the administrative border of the city, as the base for 'one-city development'—the prime goal for the planning of metropolitan circles (see Chapter 2). Based on this commuting circle, a spatial and planning concept of Greater Shanghai metropolitan circle has been imagined, containing Shanghai and major cities surrounding it: Suzhou, Wuxi, Changzhou, and Nantong in Jiangsu province; and Jiaxing, Ningbo, Zhoushan, and Huzhou in Zhejiang province (see Figure 4.4).

This Greater Shanghai metropolitan circle covers a land area of 56,000 km^2 and had a population of around 71 million and regional GDP of around RMB 10 trillion (USD 1.57 trillion) (SHPNRB, 2020). If this were a country, its population would rank 20th, sitting between Germany and France (Wikipedia, 2022a), and its GDP 14th between Australia and Spain (Wikipedia, 2022b).

72 *The dragon's head in spatial imaginary*

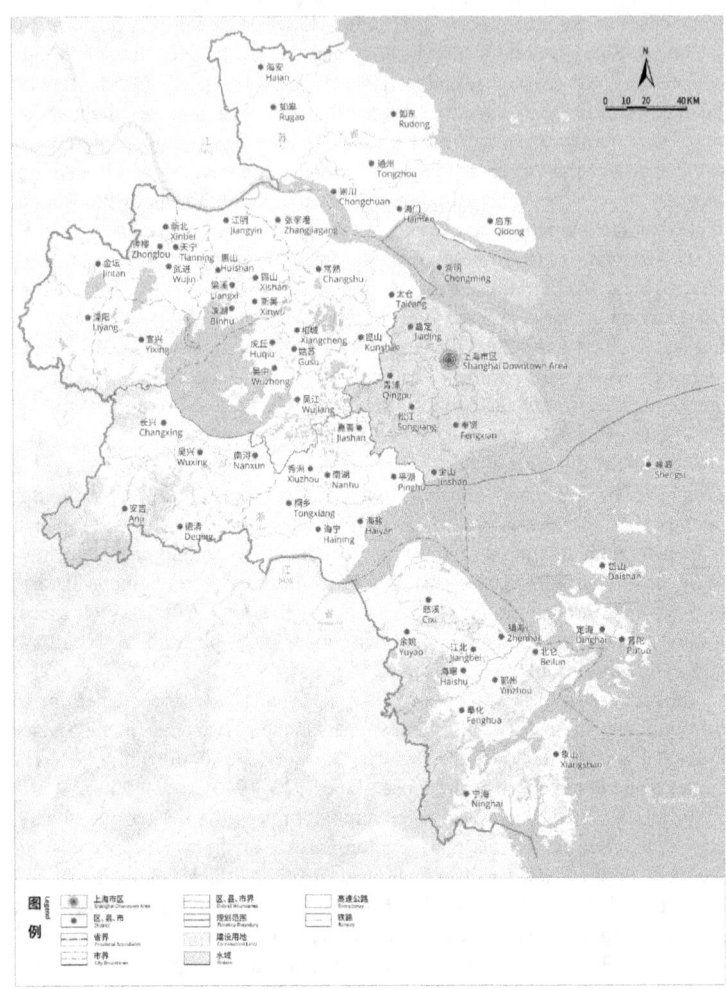

Figure 4.4 Greater Shanghai metropolitan circle
Source: Shanghai Government et al. (2022).

The Shanghai government took the lead in formulating the *Spatial Coordinative Plan for the Greater Shanghai Metropolitan Circle* for this metropolitan circle in collaboration with the governments of Jiangsu and Zhejiang provinces. Released in September 2022, this spatial plan outlines a vision of 'excellent global city region' (Shanghai Government et al., 2022), an extension of the 'excellent global city' vision set in *Shanghai 2035*. This Greater Shanghai metropolitan circle plan boasts of being the first territorial spatial plan across provinces created under the new territorial spatial planning system that started in 2019 (see Chapter 2).

The spatial imaginary of Greater Shanghai metropolitan circle has emerged in the new context of China's regional planning and development. The concept was first mentioned in the State Council's approval letter for *Shanghai 2035*, pointing out the necessity of enhancing the interaction between Shanghai and its surrounding cities to forge such a Greater Shanghai metropolitan circle. In the 2019 *Outline Plan for Integrated Development of the Yangtze River Delta Region*, the notion was raised again. Even though the making of a territorial spatial plan for this metropolitan circle was bottom-up, the imagining of the concept was top-down.

The Greater Shanghai metropolitan circle, as a spatial imaginary, reflects Shanghai's role as the dragon's head in the region. Geospatially, it seems a meso-region sitting between the Yangtze River delta city cluster and the distinct metropolitan circles mapped out for the region (see Figure 4.1). It incorporates the whole Suzhou-Wuxi-Changzhou metropolitan circle and parts of the Hangzhou and Ningbo metropolitan circles. This Greater Shanghai metropolitan circle seems to impose a 'super metropolitan circle' on the existing ones with Shanghai as the central city (Hu, 2023b, p. 135).

The imaginary of Greater Shanghai metropolitan circle has been driven by a need for regional interaction and coordination. Its spatial scoping is both bold and compromised (see Figure 4.4). It includes major cities that are leading not only in the region but in the nation, as stated earlier. It intentionally does not include Hangzhou—an important city in its own right—but includes Jiaxing and Huzhou, the member cities of the Hangzhou metropolitan circle. It also includes Ningbo and Zhoushan, which are further away from Shanghai than Hangzhou.

There are important administrative factors in this spatial imaginary for regional planning: presumably, the inventors for the Greater Shanghai metropolitan circle do not want to challenge the status of Hangzhou as the provincial capital of Zhejiang through excluding it out of its spatial scope. Paradoxically, regional planning is premised on a need to address these administrative factors. In regional planning, there is often a discrepancy between where the boundary is drawn in practice and how the region is defined in conception.

The Greater Shanghai metropolitan circle aims to streamline the spatial imaginary for the region led by the dragon's head. Ironically, it also seems to be complicating the regional planning by creating a new layer of spatial imaginary and resultant confusion.

Minding the imaginary-practice gap

When cities are chained into megaregions, regional coordination becomes a paramount planning and governance issue. There are two overarching goals in all the efforts to achieve integrated regional development. One is to break through the administrative borders and associated governance, planning, services, and infrastructure that are all 'bordered'. The other is to rebalance the centrality of urban functions, capacities, and resources that are 'overconcentrated' in those central cities.

However, the primacy and operationalisation of these goals vary by megaregion. For the Beijing-Tianjin-Hebei region, the overconcentration seems a more acute issue than in the Yangtze River delta region. In the former, decentralisation—relocating those non-capital functions out of Beijing—is the focal planning approach (see Chapter 2). In the latter, spill-overs from Shanghai have shaped the regional planning thinking. The decentralisation of Beijing has been pushed by a strong political will and is under top-down intervention. The dragon's head role of Shanghai seems to be playing out mostly through market forces and bottom-up initiatives, boosted by a top-down elevation of the development of Yangtze River delta region into a national strategy. These do not just reflect the nuances in the planning approaches of the two megaregions. They have been in the DNA of these two megaregions: Beijing's dominance in the region has been an outcome of political factors while Shanghai's rise and its dragon's head role have clear geospatial and economic logics.

All the discussed regional plans converge on one central objective of achieving integrated development that breaks through the administrative borders between cities and between provinces. This is a challenge confronting regional planning in China and elsewhere, and there is no easy approach or panacea that would work for all regions. The Yangtze River delta region is not short of plans of various types and at various scales, combining both top-down and bottom-up efforts. While they aim at integrated regional development, the integration of these plans presents a planning management issue. The inter-plan relationship exists both horizontally and vertically. In the new Chinese planning system, a regional plan is an 'articulator' plan (see Chapter 2). The implementation of a regional plan highly relies on how it articulates with other plans, especially those plans that have statutory status. A considerable gap exists between the multi-scalar imaginaries and the implementation of them in practice. This gap does not apply to the Yangtze River delta region only; it is a common issue in achieving integrated regional planning and development.

References

Chinese Government. (2019). *Outline plan for integrated development of the Yangtze River delta region*. [in Chinese]. www.gov.cn/zhengce/2019-12/01/content_5457442.htm

Hu, R. (2023a). *Reinventing the Chinese city*. Columbia University Press.

Hu, R. (2023b). Shanghai: New directions in Chinese metropolitan planning. In R. Hu (Ed.), *Routledge handbook of Asian cities* (pp. 126–139). Routledge.

Hu, R., & Chen, W. (2019). *Global Shanghai remade: The rise of Pudong new area*. Routledge. https://doi.org/10.4324/9780429316180

NDRC. (2010). *Plan for the demonstration zone of Wanjiang urban belt for accommodating industrial relocations*. [in Chinese]. https://www.gov.cn/gzdt/att/att/site1/20100324/001e3741a2cc0d13bd3c01.pdf

NDRC. (2016, 11 October). *Outline development plan for the Yangtze River economic belt formally released*. [in Chinese]. https://cjjjd.ndrc.gov.cn/gongzuodongtai/quanweifabu/guanfangfabu/201908/t20190801_943674.htm

NDRC & MHURD (Ministry for Housing and Urban-Rural Development). (2016). *Development plan for the Yangtze River delta city cluster*. [in Chinese]. NDRC. https://www.ndrc.gov.cn/xxgk/zcfb/ghwb/201606/t20160603_962187.html?code=&state=123

Shanghai Bureau of Statistics. (2021). *Shanghai statistical yearbook 2021*. [in Chinese]. https://tjj.sh.gov.cn/tjnj/nj21.htm?d1=2021tjnj/C0112.htm

Shanghai Government. (2018). *Shanghai master plan 2017–2035*. [in Chinese]. Shanghai Urban Planning and Land Resource Administration Bureau. https://www.supdri.com/2035/index.php?c=message&a=type&tid=33

Shanghai Government. (2021). *The 14th five-year plan for development of the Zhangjiang Science City of Shanghai*. [in Chinese]. https://kcb.sh.gov.cn/html/1/170/292/1880.html#anchor232

Shanghai Government, Jiangsu Government, & Zhejiang Government. (2022). *Spatial coordinative plan for the Greater Shanghai metropolitan circle*. [in Chinese]. https://www.shanghai.gov.cn/nw12344/20220928/43ffc9be207448c4b2c910c17ac02aaa.html

SHPNRB (Shanghai Planning and Natural Resources Bureau). (2020, 9 October). *Collaborative planning for the Greater Shanghai metropolitan circle*. [in Chinese]. https://ghzyj.sh.gov.cn/gzdt/20201009/3e74e232eb4f4436a3972b63e1f8adf1.html

Sohu. (2023, 10 February). *The newest top 200 Chiense cities by GDP 2022*. [in Chinese]. https://www.sohu.com/a/638952654_120636225

Songjiang Government. (2022). *G60 Innovation Corridor*. [in Chinese]. https://g60.songjiang.gov.cn/WebSite/Introduce_1.aspx

The Economist. (2023, 5 August). *An unlikely tech cluster exemplifies China's economic vision*. The Economist. https://www.economist.com/finance-and-economics/2023/08/05/an-unlikely-tech-cluster-exemplifies-chinas-economic-vision

Wikipedia. (2022a). *List of countries and dependencies by population*. https://en.wikipedia.org/wiki/List_of_countries_and_dependencies_by_population

Wikipedia. (2022b). *List of countries by GDP (nominal)*. https://en.wikipedia.org/wiki/List_of_countries_by_GDP_(nominal)

Wikipedia. (2023, 6 April). *List of prefecture-level cities in Anhui province by GDP*. [in Chinese]. https://zh.wikipedia.org/wiki/%E5%AE%89%E5%BE%BD%E5%90%84%E5%9C%B0%E7%BA%A7%E5%B8%82%E5%9C%B0%E5%8C%BA%E7%94%9F%E4%BA%A7%E6%80%BB%E5%80%BC%E5%88%97%E8%A1%A8

5 'One country, two cities'

Relational planning of Shenzhen and Hong Kong in the Greater Bay Area

Deng Xiaoping's statue stands on the top of the Lotus Hill, looking over Futian, the business and civic centre of Shenzhen. Deng is regarded as the father of Shenzhen, an urban miracle achieved through his political vision. This is a myth. As examined in my book *The Shenzhen Phenomenon* (2020), Shenzhen is both a planned and unplanned city: it originated from grassroots ingenuity and boldness, which received top-down endorsement. Of course, Deng's support was crucial for enabling the city's genesis and progress. His role was especially important when the new city—and the capitalist experiment it represented—encountered objections and obstacles during the political contests between the reformists and the conservatives in much of the 1980s and the early 1990s (Hu, 2020, pp. 27–33).

Shenzhen is more than a city made from scratch. It is symbolic of the remaking of China through Deng Xiaoping's agenda of 'reform and opening-up'. Deng visited Shenzhen twice. In January 1984, Deng first visited Shenzhen to learn about the urban experiment, which was facing criticism from conservatives and uncertainty about its future. In January 1992, Deng visited Shenzhen again in his famous Southern Tour (*nan xun*), during which he visited several southern cities and made a series of informal but strategic remarks advocating his pro-development stance. Both visits of Deng to Shenzhen were crucial for the city's development, for China's urban and economic growth and, most of all, for Deng's 'reform and opening-up' agenda.

During his second visit to Shenzhen in 1992, Deng urged Guangdong province to speed up its development and catch up with Asia's Four Little Dragons—South Korea, Taiwan, Hong Kong, and Singapore—in 20 years. In 2020, the gross domestic product (GDP) of Guangdong province surpassed that of South Korea, the largest economy of the Four Little Dragons. Guangdong is China's largest provincial economy. It contains the Greater Bay Area, one of China's economic engines and a global city region.

In 1980, the Chinese government formally designated Shenzhen as a special economic zone (SEZ)—when it was largely a vast rural land—simply for its proximity to Hong Kong. The primary consideration was to capitalise

DOI: 10.4324/9781003108405-5

on the spill-overs of investment, technology, management, talent, and market from Hong Kong, which was already a newly industrialised economy and an emerging international financial centre at that time.

More than four decades later, Shenzhen has also risen into an international metropolis. It has now surpassed Hong Kong in aggregate GDP—this was unimaginable when Shenzhen was first proposed as an SEZ. This shift in the intercity relationality is remarkable, but the contributory factors and resultant effects are complicated: many of them are beyond these two cities and involve regional, national, and international situations.

Shenzhen and Hong Kong are close, but their relationality is complex and special. They are interrelated and interdependent—geographically, economically, and functionally; they are also profoundly separated—historically, socially, and jurisdictionally. They complement, collaborate, compete, and contradict, influencing the way they have been planned in relation to each other.

Greater Bay Area: 'One country, two systems' in regional planning

Nationally and internationally, the governance structure of the Greater Bay Area is unique. The region contains cities in both Guangdong province and China's special administrative regions (SARs) of Hong Kong and Macau, which have a high degree of autonomy and are separated by a border with customs under 'one country, two systems'. Deng Xiaoping designed this policy to take over Hong Kong and Macau from colonial rule in 1997 and 1999, respectively. The considerations for the policy were complicated and strategic, aiming both to achieve national unification and to minimise disruptions to the two cities when they returned to their motherland. This governance structure presents an unusual context for regional planning and development of the Greater Bay Area.

The Greater Bay Area contains an urban structure of '2 + 9': two SARs of Hong Kong and Macau and nine cities in Guangdong province—Guangzhou, Shenzhen, Zhuhai, Foshan, Huizhou, Dongguan, Zhongshan, Jiangmen, and Zhaoqing (see Figure 5.1). The area had a total population of 71 million, a total GDP of US$1,643 billion, and GDP per capita of US$23,400 as of the end of 2018 (HKSARG, 2018). Overseas counterpart regions like the New York megaregion, the San Francisco Bay Area, and the Greater Tokyo Area are frequently used to analogise and benchmark the planning imaginary and practice for the Greater Bay Area. At home, when compared with the Yangtze River delta region and the Beijing–Tianjin–Heibei region, the Greater Bay Area is generally perceived as the most open and dynamic. It has important historical and contemporary attributes that the other two regions do not have: it has Hong Kong and Macau, and because of them, Shenzhen and Zhuhai were designated as SEZs, spearheading China's 'reform and opening-up' from the early 1980s.

78 *'One country, two cities'*

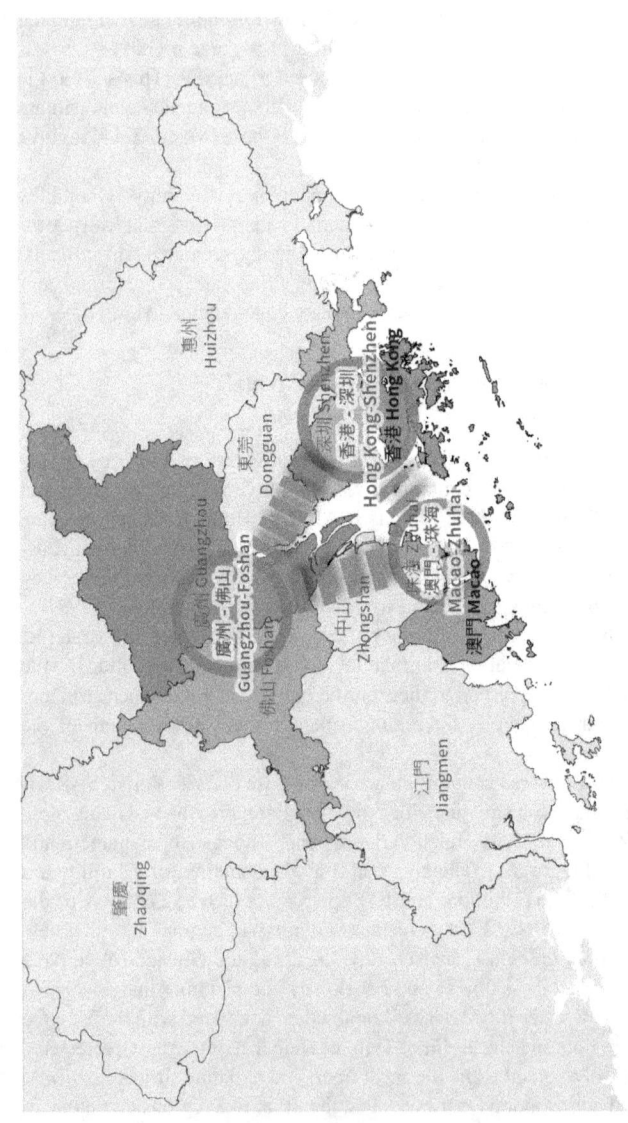

Figure 5.1 Greater Bay Area
Source: HKSARG (2021a).

'One country, two systems' has been a major factor in the imaginary and practice of regionwide planning and development of the Greater Bay Area. Formalised regional initiatives were first made for economic development in the 2000s. In 2003, the Closer Economic Partnership Arrangement (CEPA) was established between Hong Kong and the mainland. In 2008, the central government promulgated the *Outline Plan for the Reform and Development of the Pearl River Delta (2008–2020)*. The former was a free trade agreement, and the latter was a regional plan. Both were milestone initiatives to support and enable regional economic cooperation and integration under a 'collaborative governance regime' framework (Cheung, 2015, p. 1916).

From the mid-2010s, both the regional initiatives and the governance regime for the Greater Bay Area have been changing. There are two contextual factors for the changes. One is the ascendance of regional planning and the elevation of the development of the trio of megaregions—the Beijing–Tianjin–Hebei region, Yangtze River delta region, and Greater Bay Area—into national strategies (see Chapters 1, 2, and 4). The other is that the 'one country, two systems' policy is in transition as well, responding to the shifting power relations between the mainland and Hong Kong, and the complexities in local politics in Hong Kong and in broader geopolitics (Hu, 2023a). Both factors have led to the central government's strengthened involvement in the planning of the Greater Bay Area in the recent decade.

On 1 July 2017, the 20th anniversary of Hong Kong's return, Xi Jinping attended the signing of the *Framework Agreement on Deepening Guangdong–Hong Kong–Macau Cooperation in Development of the Greater Bay Area*. It was signed by four parties—the National Development and Reform Commission (NDRC), the Guangdong government, and the SAR governments of Hong Kong and Macau—representing the central government and the three provincial/SAR-level governments. This agreement signified a 'deepened' intervention by the central government into the planning of the Greater Bay Area and into the integration of the two SARs with the region and the mainland.

On 18 February 2019, the State Council promulgated the *Outline Plan for Development of the Guangdong–Hong Kong–Macau Greater Bay Area*. The most prominent feature of this outline plan is its explicit, assertive inclusion of Hong Kong and Macau under the Greater Bay Area's planning framework and further the integration of them with national development. The plan identifies four central cities—Hong Kong, Macau, Guangzhou, and Shenzhen—as the engines of the region, and differentiates the strategic roles of Hong Kong (as an international metropolis of finance, logistics, trade, and advanced services) and Shenzhen (as a national economic centre and an innovative, creative metropolis with world influence).

The *14th Five-Year Plan* (2021–2025) further affirms the central government's will to strengthen the competitive advantages of Hong Kong and Macau and to integrate them into the national development pattern (Chinese Government, 2021, pp. 136–137). To achieve these, the plan includes multiple regional development initiatives and intercity collaborations between Shenzhen and Hong Kong and between Zhuhai and Macau in the future.

The central government's growing intervention into the regional planning aims at 'killing two birds with one stone': to develop the Greater Bay Area into a world-class region to enhance national competitiveness; and to reorient Hong Kong and Macau towards regional integration and national development under 'one country, two systems', which has been significantly reinterpreted by the central government to justify its 'overall jurisdiction' (*quan mian guan zhi quan*) over the SARs. The most drastic change to 'one country, two systems' has occurred after the 2019 street movement in Hong Kong: the central government imposed a national security law in 2020 and changed the SAR's electoral system in 2021, which represent 'the most fundamental transformation of Hong Kong's governance' since its return to China in 1997 (Hu, 2023b, p. 184).

An understanding of the Shenzhen–Hong Kong relationality and an integrated planning approach to the Greater Bay Area must be situated under the region's governance structure of 'one country, two systems', which is also experimental, evolving, and changing. This governance structure creates a unique situation of 'one country, two cities' for understanding the relational planning of Shenzhen and Hong Kong.

Hong Kong in the planning of Shenzhen: From depending on to supporting

Hong Kong has always been a prime factor in the planning of Shenzhen. However, the nature of the Hong Kong factor and its effect on Shenzhen's planning have been changing, along with the two cities' respective development trajectories, the shift in their relationality, and changing national and international contexts. The changes are clearly reflected in the several master plans for Shenzhen released in 1986, 1996, and 2010 as well as the latest master plan *Shenzhen 2035* released for public consultation in 2021.

The 1986 plan outlined a spatial structure for Shenzhen SEZ, which was anchored along the border with Hong Kong. Shenzhen's connection with Hong Kong determined the layout of the urban structure. The earliest development precinct was planned in Luohu only because of its proximity to Hong Kong and a customs port located there. In 1984, Deng Xiaoping described SEZs as a 'window' to technology, knowledge, management, and the opening-up policy (Deng, 1993, pp. 51–52). This 'window' concept had a strong impact on the early planning and development of Shenzhen. For Shenzhen, this 'window' was opened to Hong Kong, and to the world via Hong Kong. Indeed, Hong Kong was the reason for Shenzhen becoming an SEZ. Compared to the other three SEZs—Zhuhai, Shantou, and Xiamen—established at the same time, Shenzhen has grown the fastest and is the most successful. Many factors could explain Shenzhen's growth and success, but the Hong Kong factor should be the most important one. It is no wonder that the 1986 plan, and the planning efforts preceding and following it, had a strong tendency to capitalise on the Hong Kong opportunities. This planning tendency resonated with Shenzhen's development: its manufacturing economy and property development were mostly Hong Kong-related in the 1980s.

The 1996 plan set the vision of 'a modern international metropolis' for Shenzhen and covered a citywide planning area that was wider than the SEZ delineated in the 1986 plan (Shenzhen Government, 1996). The 1996 plan expressed three major dimensions of the Shenzhen–Hong Kong connection: national mission of 'one country, two systems', infrastructure connection, and economic connection. For the first dimension, Hong Kong's return to China in 1997 presented a new context for imagining the Shenzhen–Hong Kong connection: Shenzhen was tasked with a national mission of 'providing structural preparation for ensuring Hong Kong's prosperity and stability' (Shenzhen Government, 1996). Both 'prosperity' and 'stability' are the key concepts in the Chinese discourse of Hong Kong affairs before and after its return (Hu, 2023a, p. 41). This mission seemed prescient about Hong Kong's economic fluctuation and political turmoil after its handover to China. Because of this mission, the 1996 plan, for the first time in Shenzhen's planning history, explicitly articulated the city's role in fulfilling the 'one country, two systems' policy and national unification.

The second dimension of the Shenzhen–Hong Kong connection related to the transport infrastructure—land, sea, and air—connecting the two cities and connecting Hong Kong to the mainland via Shenzhen. The third dimension of the Shenzhen–Hong Kong connection was their economic complementarity. This intercity complementarily was built upon the economic interdependence between Hong Kong and both the Greater Bay Area and the mainland in the late 20th century. Hong Kong, as an international finance and trade centre, served the role of providing foreign direct investment (FDI) and transferring international trade for the mainland, while its manufacturing sectors were relocated offshore mainly to the Greater Bay Area (Ramon-Berjano et al., 2011). In the mid-1990s, Shenzhen's economic base remained industrial, complementing Hong Kong's post-industrial economy.

The 2010 plan took an active, and even assertive, stance on the Shenzhen–Hong Kong cooperation. It defined one major function of Shenzhen as 'a servicing base of the national support for Hong Kong's prosperity and stability; and an international finance, trade, and shipping centre co-developing with Hong Kong under the framework of "one country, two systems"'; it also set one vision of 'strengthening the Shenzhen–Hong Kong cooperation and co-building a world-class metropolitan region' (Shenzhen Government, 2010, p. 3). These 'co-developing' and 'co-building' expressions denoted a balance, or equal weighting, between the two cities, which would have been unimaginable three decades ago when Shenzhen was an embryonic SEZ.

The 2010 plan outlined seven areas for strengthening the Shenzhen–Hong Kong cooperation: finance, innovation, business services, airports, cross-border connection, cross-border joint development, and ecological and environmental protection and management. The first three areas concerned Shenzhen's economic transformation towards a knowledge economy—one key theme of the 2010 plan—through cooperating with Hong Kong, a leading global centre in these areas. The prominence of the Shenzhen–Hong Kong cooperation in the 2010 plan reflected an imperative for Shenzhen's economic transformation towards a knowledge economy on the one hand. On the other hand, it reflected a strong aspiration, from the Shenzhen side at least, for closer economic collaboration with Hong Kong. This aspiration emerged in the circumstance that Hong Kong experienced economic fluctuations in most of the period after its return in 1997. At the same time, the central government, in large part through Guangdong province and Shenzhen, adopted a series of measures, including CEPA, which aimed to support Hong Kong's economic resurrection but led to undesired outcomes of social conflicts and political repercussions in Hong Kong, however (Hu, 2023a, pp. 44–46).

In June 2021, a draft master plan—*Shenzhen 2035*—was released for public consultation. This draft plan covers the timeframe 2020–2035. The public consultation process has concluded. Somehow, the plan had not been officially released as of January 2024. Presumably, the vision and goals in the final version will not be significantly different from those in the draft version. *Shenzhen 2035* was made after China's new territorial spatial planning system was in place in 2019 (see Chapter 2), as reflected in the plan's full title *Shenzhen 2035: Territorial Spatial Master Plan of Shenzhen*.

In *Shenzhen 2035*, the city is commissioned with both an urban vision and a political mission—advancing Chinese urban development approach and showcasing Chinese socialism—and it is expected to become a Chinese model city and a global benchmark city in the coming decades (SZPNRB, 2021, p. 3). This sounds confident—if not complacent—and clearly reflects the changing political culture and growing nationalism and their influences on the Chinese planning discourse. The recent master plans for major cities like Shenzhen, Beijing, and Shanghai, which are all aligned to the national development strategy towards 2035 (see Chapter 1), reflect the new directions in Chinese metropolitan planning as well as the political influences of Xi Jinping's 'new era' on urban imaginary (Hu, 2023c, pp. 130–134).

'Support' is the key concept underpinning the Hong Kong (and Macau) narrative in *Shenzhen 2035*:

> Support the fusion of Hong Kong and Macau into the national development megatrend: expand and deepen Shenzhen–Hong Kong–Macau cooperation in multiple areas in an all-round manner; support Hong Kong's economic and social development…
>
> (SZPNRB, 2021, p. 6)

'One country, two cities' 83

This narrative is unsurprising in light of the timing of the plan's production. It was produced after Hong Kong experienced the most transformative years of 2019–2021.

Shenzhen in the planning of Hong Kong: From division to fusion

Before Hong Kong's return to China in 1997, its planning was independent in terms of both jurisdiction and regional planning thinking. This was in contrast to Hong Kong's role in the planning of Shenzhen, which had placed Hong Kong in a very important position, as examined above. In the early years after Hong Kong's return, in both conception and practice, Shenzhen was not a major factor in Hong Kong's strategic planning. But the change has been accelerating in the recent decade, and drastically in recent years.

Hong Kong 2030 (2007) was the city's first strategic plan after its return. The plan set the long-term vision of 'Asia's world city', which is still the city's slogan today. The plan acknowledged the new circumstance of the city's reunification with the motherland and incorporated the national dimension—the national five-year plan, cross-border connections, and the Greater Bay Area—into the envisioning of the plan. As a result, both Shenzhen and the Greater Bay Area stood out in the plan's spatial imaginary for Hong Kong's future.

The plan identified a Northern Development Axis (see Figure 5.2) as one of the preferred development options for 'non-intensive technology and business zones and other uses that capitalise on the strategic advantage of the boundary location' (HKSARG, 2007, p. 125). The plan clearly considered the city's integration with Shenzhen in the future roadmap:

> [The area next to Shenzhen] presents itself as a rare development opportunity. It offers good potential for commercial and high-tech development that would benefit Hong Kong's economy, making use of its strategic locational advantages to provide space for better integration between Shenzhen and Hong Kong.
>
> (HKSARG, 2007, pp. 192–193)

The plan also considered the development of the Greater Bay Area and the necessity of facilitating it into 'one region':

> In the context of the evolution of the PRD [Pearl River Delta] Region as a multi-centred city-region, Hong Kong needs to recognise the synergy of co-operation and coordination.... Maintaining a close relation with our most immediate neighbours, Shenzhen, Macao and Zhuhai, is of particular importance. We must recognise that as they make further progress in their

84 *'One country, two cities'*

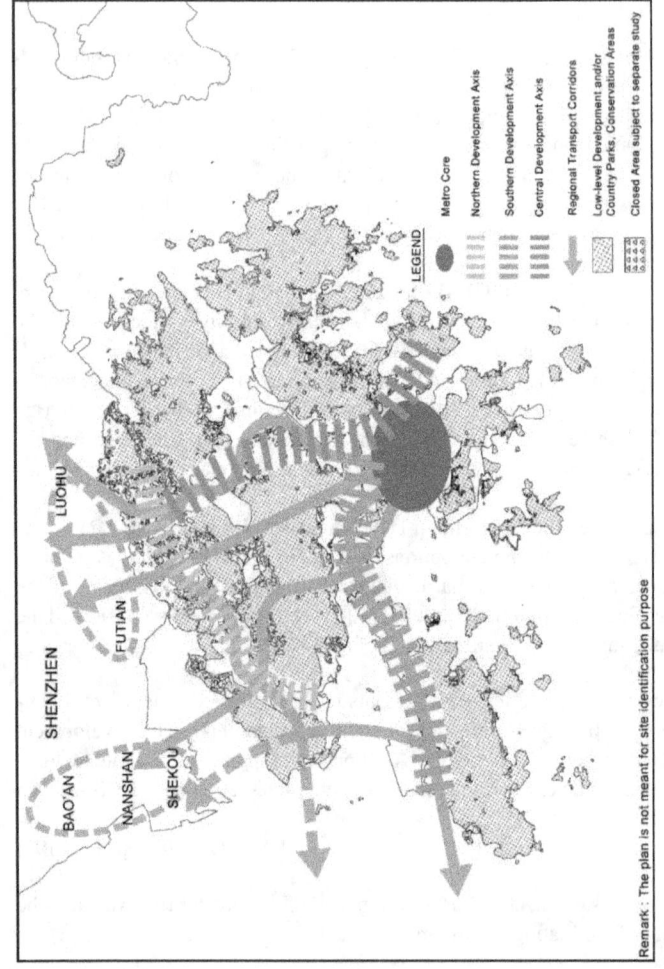

Figure 5.2 Strategic concept plan for *Hong Kong 2030*
Source: HKSARG (2007).

development, our differences will become increasingly obscure. From the socio-economic angle, it is not unrealistic to assume that all could become one within the next decade or so.

(HKSARG, 2007, p. 195)

In 2016, an updated plan *Hong Kong 2030+* was produced for public engagement. In its conceptual spatial framework, it identified a Northern Economic Belt for 'potential for warehousing, R&D [research and development] and modern logistics capitalising on the strategic location for being in close proximity to Shenzhen' (HKSARG, 2016, p. 64).

The boldest spatial imaginary along the border with Shenzhen came in 2021. On 6 October, Chief Executive Carrie Lam presented her policy address Building a Bright Future Together, the last one in her term of office 2017–2022, but the first one after the city experienced the 2019 street movement and subsequent national security law and new electoral system. Among many initiatives that were explicitly aligned to national development strategies and to integration with Shenzhen and the Greater Bay Area, the most prominent one was a proposed Northern Metropolis. On the same day, the *Northern Metropolis Development Strategy* was also released.

The Northern Metropolis is a significant step up from the previous 2007 Northern Development Axis and 2016 Northern Economic Belt in terms of spatial imaginary:

> By taking advantage of its geographical proximity to Shenzhen, the [Northern Metropolis] Development Strategy promotes Hong Kong's integration into the overall development of our country and the [GBA] Greater Bay Area. By leveraging the strengths of integration with Shenzhen, the Northern Metropolis will be developed into the second engine of economic growth of Hong Kong and a promising metropolitan area to live in, work and travel.
>
> (HKSARG, 2021b, p. 11)

The Northern Metropolis is a 20-year initiative, covering an area of 300 km² in north Hong Kong along the border with Shenzhen and accommodating some 2.5 million people and 650,000 jobs including 150,000 information technology jobs (HKSARG, 2021b, p. 76). The future of the Northern Metropolis will be an innovation and technology hub, complementing the Harbour Metropolis in the southern part, which is an established leading international financial hub. The proposed Northern Metropolis was incorporated into the *Hong Kong 2030+* strategy, profoundly reshaping the city's conceptual spatial framework (Figure 5.3).

Indeed, the Northern Metropolis is a bold, ambitious blueprint, reorienting Hong Kong's development through boosting Hong Kong–Shenzhen integration and capitalising on the spill-overs from Shenzhen, which is

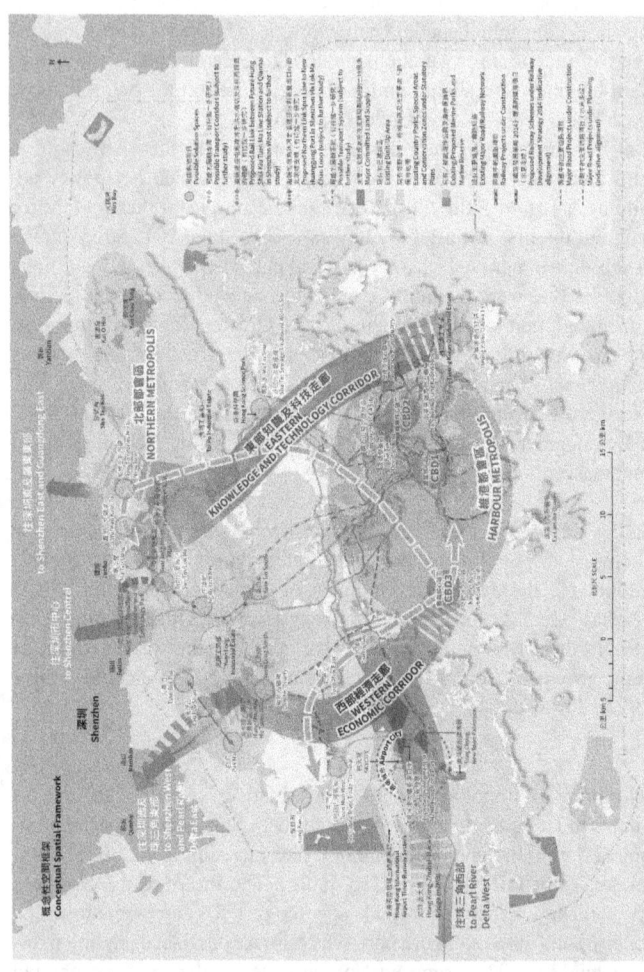

Figure 5.3 Conceptual spatial framework for *Hong Kong 2030+*
Source: HKSARG (2021a).

already an innovation centre of global leadership. Form the Hong Kong side, it marks a significant change from division to fusion in the intercity relational planning.

Relational shifts

The recent changes in the relational planning of both Shenzhen and Hong Kong challenge the previous readings of their relationship. These readings include, for example, that they are not twin cities and are way from that direction (Bontje, 2019; Shen, 2014); and that they have followed diverging planning cultures and development trajectories in a co-existence across the boundary (Ng, 2005). These readings were established on the old contexts and practices which have significantly changed in recent years, turning from bifurcating to converging towards integration and fusion in terms of relational planning and intercity development. The *Northern Metropolis Development Strategy* (2021) has one chapter exclusively on 'Hong Kong–Shenzhen crossboundary strategic spatial framework', signifying a relational shift from 'two bays, one river', which divide the two cities, to 'two cities, three circles', which fuse their development (HKSARG, 2021b, p. 25). This relational shift in spatial imaginary has underlying economic and political causes.

Investment and GDP are the key economic indicators to measure the shifts in the relationality between Shenzhen and Hong Kong. One important role played by Hong Kong in Shenzhen's growth is investment, which is classified as FDI under 'one country, two systems'. Nearly 70 per cent of Shenzhen's cumulative FDI came from Hong Kong (and Macau) in 1987–2017, and the remaining 30 per cent was split among a group of countries/regions with a very small proportion for each (Shenzhen Statistical Bureau, 2018). This predominance of Hong Kong FDI applies not only to Shenzhen, but also to the whole mainland. By September 2017, 52.6 per cent of the cumulative FDI that was actually used in the mainland came from Hong Kong; the annual share of Hong Kong's FDI in the mainland fluctuated between 30 per cent and 70 per cent in most of these years (Chen, 2019). As is commonly known, FDI has played a significant role in China's rapid economic growth and urbanisation. It is fair to say that Hong Kong's contribution to China's economic rise was utmost, in the early stages especially.

Not all the Hong Kong FDI in Shenzhen and the mainland was local funds. A considerable amount of the investment was made by Hong Kong-based subsidiaries of overseas companies (Chen, 2019). It is also counted as FDI from Hong Kong as the source region. This gateway role of Hong Kong—being a conduit linking China and the world—was no less important than Hong Kong's local resources of capital and expertise in supporting China's opening and growth. The cultural kinship and geographical proximity put Hong Kong's businesses in an advantageous position to first enter China. Their success in China also set an example for international investors who were uncertain and hesitant in the early stages of China's 'reform and opening-up'. Shenzhen has thus enjoyed the most convenience in receiving the local opportunities from Hong Kong and those overseas opportunities transmitted through Hong Kong.

This economic relationship is not one-way, but rather reciprocal. Hong Kong FDI also capitalised on the opportunities from China's 'reform and opening-up'. Hong Kong's economy was industrialised from the 1950s, which turned the city into an economic powerhouse; the economy was further tertiarised, turning the city into a financial centre from the 1970s (Ng, 2005). The mainland's open-door policy was timely for Hong Kong's economic transformation. Those labour-intensive manufacturing sectors were shifted to Shenzhen and inland cities, and thus helped transition Hong Kong from an industrial to post-industrial economy and establish it as a leading global financial centre (Ramon-Berjano et al., 2011).

This reciprocity between Hong Kong as an international gateway and the mainland as a hinterland structured their economic relationship in much of the 1980s and 1990s. In the 21st century, the one-way investment from Hong Kong to China was increasingly replaced by two-way investment between them. Hong Kong became the primary destination of China's investment overseas, along with the rise of the national economy (Chen, 2019). This mutual investment and other economic activities, including trade and visitors, have redefined the relationality between Hong Kong and Shenzhen (and the mainland) in the 21st century.

The relationality with Hong Kong has spurred Shenzhen's growth, which has further shifted this relationality. Several measures help illustrate the rapid growth of Shenzhen in comparison with Hong Kong. Shenzhen's labour force and population overtook Hong Kong's in 1996 and 2000, respectively (Duhalde, 2018). The economic shift, however, deserves the most attention. In 1979, Shenzhen's GDP was negligible and accounted for only 0.09 per cent of Hong Kong's; in 2017, Shenzhen's GDP surpassed Hong Kong's for the first time (Figure 5.4). Measured by GDP per capita, the gap between these two cities has been narrowing: in 1979, Hong Kong's GDP per capita was 53 times of Shenzhen's; in 2020, Shenzhen's GDP per capita was 74 per cent of Hong Kong's (Figure 5.4). One factor explaining the difference in GDP per capita between Shenzhen and Hong Kong is their population difference. In 2023, Shenzhen's population was 13 million (World Population Review, 2023b); Hong Kong's was 7.5 million (World Population Review, 2023a). Their gap in GDP per capita also reflects the qualitative difference between their economies: the Hong Kong's economy remains more advanced and productive although the Shenzhen's economy is rapidly catching up and outperforms in aggregation.

Hong Kong's economy, measured by GDP and GDP per capita, has followed a generally upward trend, which, however, has been outpaced by Shenzhen's (Figure 5.4). The faster growth of Shenzhen explains its overtaking of Hong Kong in GDP and their shrinking gap in GDP per capita. The faster

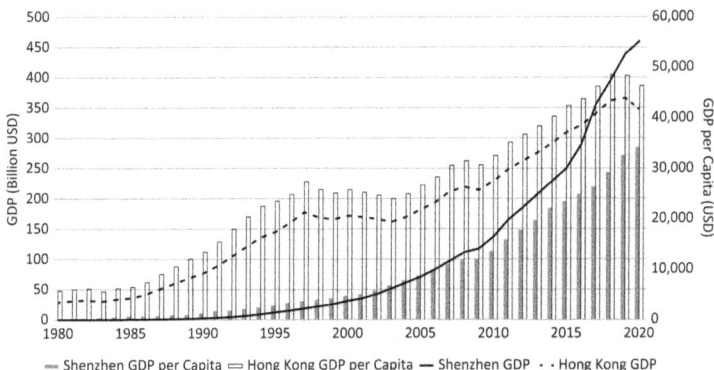

Figure 5.4 GDP of Shenzhen and Hong Kong, 1980–2020

Data source: CEIC (2022), Duhalde (2018), Lyttle (2021), Statista (2022), and the World Bank (2022), created by the author.

growth of the mainland also explains the relative decline of Hong Kong's weighting in the national economy. In 1997, when Hong Kong returned to China, its GDP share was 18.4 per cent, and it plummeted to only 2.1 per cent in 2021 (Bajpai, 2023).

In around four decades, Shenzhen's economy, starting from scratch and largely through benefiting from Hong Kong's spill-overs, has caught up even outperformed in certain aspects. This relational shift within such a short timeframe is phenomenal. The comparison and the contrast between these two cities, situated in such a unique relationality, are not paralleled by any other two cities in the world. Here, the relational shift is measured economically. But the process has involved profound political, social, and cultural shifts. These shifts have been embedded not only in the relationality of these two cities but also in the regional planning of the Greater Bay Area and the transition of 'one country, two systems'.

The *yin-yang* of Shenzhen–Hong Kong relationality

Seemingly, 'one country, two systems' is a compromised policy design. In certain aspects, it is a compromise—a pragmatic compromise considering the situations of the city, the country, and the world at the time of its design. But it is also innovative and strategic. When Deng Xiaoping designed 'one country, two systems' for Hong Kong's governance after its return and promised a 50-year tenure for it, he did not just aim at national unification. He had another important goal—his modernisation agenda of 'reform and opening-up'—for this policy design. Hong Kong played a critically important role in China's opening-up before and after its return. This role was arguably the most important in the early stage of Deng's 'reform and opening-up'. China opened its door, first and foremost, to Hong Kong.

Deng Xiaoping wanted more than one Hong Kong; he wanted several 'Hong Kongs'. On 3 June 1988, Deng met the delegates of an international conference on 'China and the World in the 1990s', and he talked about the importance of learning from international experience and his policy on Hong Kong:

> For the Hong Kong policy, we promise that it won't change for 50 years after 1997. This promise is serious. Why do we say it should not change for 50 years? There are reasons. It doesn't just mean to comfort Hong Kongers but considers the close connection between Hong Kong's prosperity and stability and China's development strategy. China's development strategy needs time. Apart from the remaining 12 years in this century, it needs 50 years in the next century. Then, how can we change [the Hong Kong policy]? Now, there is one Hong Kong. We will build several more 'Hong Kongs' in the mainland. That is to say, to achieve our strategic goals of development, we will open up even more.
>
> (Deng, 1993, p. 267)

The idea of building several 'Hong Kongs' never wavered in Deng's mind. On 31 May 1989—when the Tiananmen Square movement was on, and Deng had just changed the central government's leadership—Deng told his newly appointed leaders:

> I previously said that we need to build several more 'Hong Kongs'. That is to say, we need to open up, not withdraw, and we need to open up more than before. We cannot develop without opening up.
>
> (Deng, 1993, p. 297)

Has China built several more 'Hong Kongs'? In 2022, six mainland cities surpassed Hong Kong in GDP: Shanghai, Beijing, Shenzhen, Chongqing, Guangzhou, and Suzhou. Hong Kong, despite being a leading global city, is being challenged and surpassed by these rising mainland cities and, most importantly, by its neighbouring city Shenzhen.

No intercity relationship is as unique as Shenzhen and Hong Kong's; no intercity change is as drastic as theirs. Their difference, interdependence, and interchange in terms of 'one country, two cities' are remindful of the ancient Chinese wisdom of *yin-yang*—a world view and a methodology about understanding 'the relationality of opposite elements in a paradox' (Hu, 2020, p. 107).

In the relational planning of the two cities, there has been a *yin-yang* shift from the Hong Kong-led 'internationalisation' of Shenzhen to the Shenzhen-led 'nationalisation' of Hong Kong. The power relations driving this shift are multi-scalar: intercity, regional, national, and international. The rise of Shenzhen—and further of the Greater Bay Area and the mainland—and the relative decline of Hong Kong have underpinned the increasing integration of Hong Kong into the regional and national development patterns. This integration has been escalating in the recent decade.

There are also international factors in this process. Hong Kong, the East-West connector previously, has become a battleground of geopolitical confrontation between China and the West in recent years. The international situation today is profoundly different from that of the early 1980s. At that time, Shenzhen was in its early stage of development, largely through accessing the international opportunities coming from or transferred via Hong Kong. For a long time, even in the decades before China's opening-up, Hong Kong had been China's window to knowing and accessing the world. That window role has been significantly lessened, with the rise of China and Chinese cities—several more 'Hong Kongs' as advocated by Deng Xiaoping. Further, confronting increasing hostility and threat from the West, China is turning inward in its development strategy, prioritising 'internal circulation' over 'international circulation' in its economic development strategy (see Chapter 3). These macroenvironmental changes have also facilitated the increasing 'nationalisation' of Hong Kong's development orientation and strategy.

The unique border between Shenzhen and Hong Kong under 'one country, two systems' is both dividing and fusing in the relational planning of the two cities. 'Border' is both a noun and a verb: it is constructed, reconstructed, and deconstructed, pending structural power relations across and beyond the border. In 1980, an SEZ was imagined in Shenzhen along the border; in 2021, a Northern Metropolis was imagined in Hong Kong along the border. What a *yin-yang* in the relational planning!

References

Bajpai, P. (2023, 27 July). *Hong Kong vs mainland China: Understanding the economic and financial differences*. https://www.investopedia.com/articles/investing/121814/hong-kong-vs-china-understand-differences.asp

Bontje, M. (2019). Hong Kong and Shenzhen: Twins, rivals or potential megacity? In J. Garrard & E. Mikhailova (Eds.), *Twin cities: Urban communities, borders and relationships over time* (pp. 132–146). Routledge.

CEIC. (2022). *GDP: per capita: Guangdong: Shenzhen*. https://www.ceicdata.com/en/china/gross-domestic-product-prefecture-level-city-per-capita/cn-gdp-per-capita-guangdong-shenzhen

Chen, D. (Ed.). (2019). *40-year reform and opening-up and Hong Kong*. [in Chinese]. Joint Publishing.

Cheung, P. T. Y. (2015). Toward collaborative governance between Hong Kong and mainland China. *Urban Studies, 52*(10), 1915–1933. https://doi.org/10.1177/0042098014548139

Chinese Government. (2021). *The People's Republic of China's 14th five-year plan for national economic and social development and outline objectives of the 2035 vision*. [in Chinese]. NDRC. http://www.gov.cn/xinwen/2021-03/13/content_5592681.htm

Deng, X. (1993). *Selected works of Deng Xiaoping* (Vol. 3). [in Chinese]. People's Publishing House.

Duhalde, M. (2018, 4 December). A tale of two cities: Shenzhen vs Hong Kong. *South China Morning Post*. https://multimedia.scmp.com/news/china/article/2176135/shenzhen-hongkong/index.html

HKSARG. (2016). *Hong Kong 2030+: Towards a planning vision and strategy transcending 2030 [public engagement]*. The Development Bureau and the Planning Department. https://www.pland.gov.hk/pland_en/p_study/comp_s/hk2030plus/document/2030+Booklet_Eng.pdf

HKSARG. (2018). *Greater Bay Area: Overview*. Constitutional and Mainland Affairs Bureau. https://www.bayarea.gov.hk/en/about/overview.html

HKSARG. (2021a). *Hong Kong 2030+: Towards a planning vision and strategy transcending 2030*. The Development Bureau and the Planning Department. https://www.pland.gov.hk/pland_en/p_study/comp_s/hk2030plus/document/2030+_booklet.pdf

HKSARG. (2021b). *Northern Metropolis development strategy*. Government Logistics Department. https://www.policyaddress.gov.hk/2021/eng/pdf/publications/Northern/Northern-Metropolis-Development-Strategy-Report.pdf

HKSARG (Hong Kong Special Administrative Region Government). (2007). *Hong Kong 2030: Planning vision and strategy*. The Development Bureau and the Planning Department. https://www.pland.gov.hk/pland_en/p_study/comp_s/hk2030/eng/finalreport/pdf/E_FR.pdf

Hu, R. (2020). *The Shenzhen phenomenon: From fishing village to global knowledge city*. Routledge. https://doi.org/10.4324/9780367815653

Hu, R. (2023a). 'One country, two systems' in transition. In A. Podger, H. S. Chan, T.-t. Su, & J. Wanna (Eds.), *Dilemmas in public management in Greater China and Australia: Rising tensions but common challenges* (pp. 37–60). ANU Press. https://doi.org/10.22459/DPMGCA.2023

Hu, R. (2023b). *Reinventing the Chinese city*. Columbia University Press. https://doi.org/10.7312/hu--21100-004

Hu, R. (2023c). Shanghai: New directions in Chinese metropolitan planning. In R. Hu (Ed.), *Routledge handbook of Asian cities* (pp. 126–139). Routledge.

Lyttle, C. (2021, 12 October). *How Shenzhen moved out of Hong Kong's shadow*. Investment Monitor. https://www.investmentmonitor.ai/features/shenzhen-moved-out-of-hong-kong-shadow/?cf-view

Ng, M. K. (2005). Planning cultures in two Chinese transitional cities: Hong Kong and Shenzhen. In B. Sanyal (Ed.), *Comparative planning cultures* (pp. 113–144). Routledge.

Ramon-Berjano, C. B., Zhao, S. X., & Ming, C. Y. (2011). Hong Kong's transformation into a service hub: Regional development within 'one country, two systems'. *Asian Survey*, *51*(4), 584–609.

Shen, J. (2014). Not quite a twin city: Cross-boundary integration in Hong Kong and Shenzhen. *Habitat International*, *42*, 138–146. https://doi.org/10.1016/j.habitatint.2013.12.003

Shenzhen Government. (1996). *Shenzhen municipal master plan (1996–2010)*. [in Chinese]. https://pnr.sz.gov.cn/ztzl/csztgh/

Shenzhen Government. (2010). *Shenzhen municipal master plan (2010–2020)*. [in Chinese]. http://www.sz.gov.cn/attachment/0/684/684608/1344759.pdf

Shenzhen Statistical Bureau. (2018). *Shenzhen statistical yearbook*. [in Chinese]. China Statistics Press. http://tjj.sz.gov.cn/attachment/0/848/848611/3085962.pdf

Statista. (2022). *Gross domestic product (GDP) in China's Greater Bay Area in 2020, by city*. https://www.statista.com/statistics/1007451/china-gross-domestic-product-gdp-of-cities-in-the-greater-bay-area/#:~:text=In%202020%2C%20the%20total%20gross,in%20the%20Greater%20Bay%20Area.

SZPNRB (Shenzhen Planning and Natural Resources Bureau). (2021). *Shenzhen 2035: Territorial spatial master plan of Shenzhen (2020–2035) (version for public consultation)*. [in Chinese]. http://www.sz.gov.cn/attachment/0/794/794784/8858881.pdf

The World Bank. (2022). *GDP per capita (current US$)—Hong Kong SAR, China*. https://data.worldbank.org/indicator/NY.GDP.PCAP.CD

World Population Review. (2023a). *Hong Kong population 2023*. https://worldpopulationreview.com/countries/hong-kong-population

World Population Review. (2023b). *Shenzhen population 2023*. https://worldpopulationreview.com/world-cities/shenzhen-population

Index

Anhui province 8, 11, 13; unbalanced development in the Yangtze River delta region 59–67
Anqing (Anhui province) 61, 63, **65**
'articulator' plan (about regional plan) 13, 19, 32–33, 74
Asia's world city (Hong Kong) 83

Beijing 8, 16–17, 54, 58, 67, 68, 82, 90; in the Beijing–Tianjin–Hebei region 21–27, 74
Beijing subcentre 23, 25; *see also* Tongzhou district
Beijing–Tianjin–Hebei region 6, 13, 17, 20, 62, 74, 79; *Outline Plan for Coordinated Development of the Beijing–Tianjin–Hebei Region* (2015) 20, **21**; planning 21–27
Belt and Road Initiative **21**, 62
big city syndrome (Beijing) **21**, 22, 24
Bohai Bay 22
bottleneck road 35, 45
broken-head road 35, 45, **55**

Cai Qi 26–27
Changsha–Zhuzhou–Xiangtan metropolitan circle 29
Changzhou (Jiangsu province) 59, 66, 67, 70, 71, 73
Chengdu 17, 54; Chengdu model 30; *see also* Chengdu–Chongqing city cluster
Chengdu metropolitan circle 13, 29; *Development Plan for the Chengdu Metropolitan Circle* 30–32, 33, 52; investment 54–55; planning 29–32
Chengdu–Chongqing city cluster 30, 32–33, 58

Chinese-style modernisation 4
Chinese-style urbanisation 2–4
Chizhou (Anhui province) 63, **65**
Chongqing 16, 17, 29, 32, 58, 90; *see also* Chengdu–Chongqing city cluster
Chuzhou (Anhui province) 63, **65**, 66
city cluster 6–8; *see also* trio of city clusters
Closer Economic Partnership Arrangement (CEPA) 79, 82
common prosperity 4
Communist Party of China (CPC) 1, 4, 8, 9, 16, 20, 27, 38, 48
connectivity (in metropolitan circles) 43–48
county 11, 19, 22, 35; county-level city 11, 35, 54
Cultural Revolution 1

dashanghai 70–71
decentralisation (of Beijing) 74
Deng Xiaoping 1; market economy 37; 'one country, two systems' and Hong Kong 77, 89–91; 'reform and opening-up' 2, 25, 76; Shenzhen 76, 80
development planning system 18–19, 20, 33; *see also* territorial spatial planning system
development zone 43, 51, 54, 55, 67; in the Hangzhou metropolitan circle 40–42
Ding Wenjiang 70–71
direct-administered municipality (DAM) 16–17
dragon's head (Shanghai) 58–74
dual circulation (Chinese economy) 37; internal circulation and international circulation 91

economic development (in metropolitan circles) 36–43; *see also* Hangzhou metropolitan circle
economics, agglomeration economics 37–39
economy: digital economy 40; formal economy and informal economy 42; knowledge economy 39, 82; regional economy 13, 22, 36–43

foreign direct investment (FDI) 81, 87–88
Four Little Dragons 77
14th Five-Year Plan (2021–2025): development planning 18; G60 Innovation Corridor 70; planning and developing megaregions 6, 8, 19, 29, 38, 45
fragmentation (of regional governance) 10–12, 36, 47, 53–54
Fuzhou 29, 30

G60 Innovation Corridor 68–70
Gang of Four 1
governance system and governance capacity (modernisation of) 2, 4
government-market relationality 12, 13, 26, 37, 38; in regional economy 41–43
Greater Bay Area 14, 18, 20, **21**, 62, 67, 76–91; *Framework Agreement on Deepening Guangdong–Hong Kong–Macau Cooperation in Development of the Greater Bay Area* (2017) 79; *Outline Plan for Development of the Guangdong–Hong Kong–Macau Greater Bay Area* (2019) 20, **21**, 79; *Outline Plan for the Reform and Development of the Pearl River Delta (2008–2020)* 79
Greater Shanghai metropolitan circle 8, 14, 70–73; *Spatial Coordinative Plan for the Greater Shanghai Metropolitan Circle* (2022) 29, 72
gross domestic product (GDP) 9, 17, 20, 21, 30; of China and the world 2–3, 36; of Greater Bay Area 76, 77, 90; of Shenzhen and Hong Kong 88–89; of trio of city clusters **21**; of Yangtze River delta region 60, **61**, 63, **65**, 66–67, 71

Guangdong province 16, 22, 76–79, 82
Guangzhou 17, 40, 77, 79, 90

Hangzhou 10–11, 17, 42, 58, 66–68, 73
Hangzhou metropolitan circle 10, 54, 55, 66, 67, 73; economic development 40–41
hard power (of transport) 13, 44, 47; *see also* soft power
Hebei province 21–22, 24, 27
Hefei 61–69; Hefei model 65
high-quality development 4, 12
high-speed rail (HSR) 17, 45, 69
Hong Kong 11, 14, 25, 76–91; in planning Shenzhen 80–83; *see also* Shenzhen–Hong Kong relationality
Hong Kong 2030 (plan) 83–84
Hong Kong 2030+ (plan) 85–86
Huzhou (Zhejiang province) 10, 40, 41, 69, 70, 71, 73

imaginary-practice gap (in regional planning and development) 73–74
imbalance: intergovernmental financial powers and financial responsibilities 13, 49–50, 52; interregional 8–10, 12, 51; intraregional 8–10, 12, 21–22, 60, 62
innovation: Hangzhou 40–41; Hong Kong 85–86; innovation asset 65, 67; innovation-led development **21**, 31, 37–38, 42, 43, 61, 65, 68, 70; place-based innovation 39, 48; Yangtze River delta region 67–70
integrated development for city clusters 19–21
integration of four rail networks 45
internet plus 37
investment (in metropolitan circles) 48–56

Jiangsu province 8, 13, 22, 29, 59, 61, 63, 65–66, 71–72
jiangzhehu 59–60
Jinhua (Zhejiang province) 68, 69
Jinniu district (Chengdu) 54–55

Lam, Carrie 85
land financing 50–51
Li Keqiang 27, 37
Li Qiang 27

96 Index

low-end population 26–27
Luohu (Shenzhen) 80

Ma'anshan (Anhui province) 63, 65–67
Macau 11, 77–80, 82, 87
Mao Zedong 1
market economy 20, 37–38; socialist market economy 37, 42; *see also* planned economy
mass entrepreneurship and innovation 37
megaregion 5–8
megaregionalisation 5–6, 8, 12, 14, 59
meso-region 73
metropolitan circle 6–8
metropolitan circles on rail 45
Ministry of Natural Resources (MNR) 18, 28, 29, 32, 33

Nanjing 8, 17, 29–30, 58–59, 61, 65–67, 70
Nantong (Jiangsu province) 71
National Development and Reform Commission (NDRC) 12, 18, 20, 28, 29, 30, 38, 45, 63, 66, 79
National New-Type Urbanisation Plan (2014–2020) 6
national policies for metropolitan circles: *Guiding Opinions on Cultivating and Developing Modern Metropolitan Circles* (2019) 8, 28, 30, 38, 44, 48; *Practical Codes for Territorial Spatial Planning of Metropolitan Circles* (2021) 8, 28–29
national transport plans: *National Outline Plan for a Comprehensive and Integrative Transport Network* (2021) 44; *Outline Plan for Building a Strong Power in Transport* (2019) 44; *Reform Plan for the Financial Responsibilities and Expenditure Responsibilities of the Central and Local Governments in Transport Areas* (2019) 53
new normal 36–37
new-type urbanisation 4–6, 12, 24
Ningbo (Zhejiang province) 66, 67, 71, 73
north-south divide (in Yangtze River delta region) 61
Northern Development Axis (Hong Kong) 83, 85

Northern Metropolis (Hong Kong) 85–87, 91
Northern Metropolis Development Strategy (2021) 85, 87

'one country, two systems' 14, **21**, 77–80, 87, 89, 91
one-city development (for metropolitan circles) 13, 28–29, 30, 40, 45, 46, 52, 54, 71
'one–two–three' goal (of national transport system) 44

People's Republic of China (PRC) 1
planned economy 20; *see also* market economy
policy 'expectation' (investment in metropolitan circles) 53
poverty belt (Hebei province) 22
prefecture-level city (PLC) 11, 35, 36, 49, 66
principal contradiction (of national development) 2, 4, 9, 12, 51
prosperity and stability (Hong Kong) 81, 92
public-private partnership (PPP) 52
Pudong (Shanghai) 25, 67
Puxi (Shanghai) 67

Quzhou (Zhejiang province) 10

reduction-based development 26–27
regional planning 73–74, 77; regional planning system 18–19
research and development (R&D) 38, 54–55, 85; R&D + manufacturing 54
Route 128 (Boston) 68

Shanghai 13, 14, 16–17, **21**, 40, 58–74
Shanghai 2035 (plan) 71–73
Shantou (Guangdong province) 80
Shaoxing (Zhejiang province) 10, 41
Shenzhen 14, 17, 25, 40, 76–91; in planning Hong Kong 83–87; *see also* Shenzhen–Hong Kong relationality
Shenzhen Phenomenon, The (book) 77
Shenzhen 2035 (plan) 80, 82
Shenzhen–Hong Kong relationality 14, 80, 89; economic shift 87–91; economic complementarity 81
Shifang (Chengdu) 54–55

Singapore 76
soft power (of transport) 13, 43, 44, 47; *see also* hard power
Songjiang district (Shanghai) 68–70
Songjiang Manifesto 70
South Korea 76
Southern Tour (Deng Xiaoping) 77
spatial imaginary 13, 14, 58–74, 83, 85, 87
spatial reductionism 63, 64
special economic zone (SEZ) 76–77, 80, 81, 91
state-owned enterprise (SOE) 22, 24, 55
sub-provincial-level city 11, 35
supply-side structural reform 37
sustainable development 4, 5
Suzhou (Jiangsu province) 17, 58, 59, 66–67, 69, 71, 90
Suzhou–Wuxi–Changzhou metropolitan circle 67, 73

Taiwan 76
tax-sharing system 49
territorial spatial planning system 18–19, 73, 82; *see also* development planning system
Three Gorges Dam 17
Tiananmen 1; Tiananmen Square movement 90
Tianjin 16–17
Tongling (Anhui province) 63, **65**
Tongzhou district (Beijing) 23, 25
top-level design 13, 23, 27, 42
transfer payment 50–53
transit: development-oriented transit (DOT) 48; human transit 44, 47, 48; transit-oriented development (TOD) 47–48, 52
trio of city clusters 20–21; *see also* Beijing–Tianjin–Hebei region; Greater Bay Area; Yangtze River delta region

urban shrinkage 26
urbanisation rate: of Chengdu metropolitan circle 30; of China and the world 2–3

vertical intergovernmental tension (investment in metropolitan circles) 53–54

Wanjiang urban belt 63–65; *Plan for Demonstration Zone of the*

Index 97

Wanjiang Urban Belt for Accommodating Industrial Relocations (2010) 63
Western Development (development program of western China) 17
Wuhan 17, 29, 58
Wuhu (Anhui province) 63, **65**, 66, 67, 69, 70
Wuxi (Jiangsu province) 59, 66, 67, 70, 71

Xi Jinping 23, 25; Beijing–Tianjin–Hebei region 26; Hong Kong 79; Shanghai 68; Xiong'an 27; Yangtze River delta region 62
Xi'an 29, 58
Xiamen (Fujian province) 80
Xiong'an 24–27; Xiong'an paradox 24
Xuancheng (Anhui province) 63, **65**, 66, 69, 70

Yangtze River city cluster 66–70; *Development Plan for the Yangtze River Delta City Cluster (2016)* 20, **21**, 40, 51
Yangtze River delta region 58–74; *Outline Plan for Integrated Development of the Yangtze River Delta Region (2019)* 20, **21**, 62, 70, 73; unbalanced development 59–66
Yangtze River economic belt 58
yin-yang 89–91

Zhangjiang Science City (Shanghai) 68
Zhejiang province 11, 13, 22, 29, 59, **61**, 63, 68, 71, 72, 73
Zhengzhou 45, 52
Zhengzhou metropolitan circle: *Development Plan for the Zhengzhou Metropolitan Circle* 46; *Spatial Plan for the Zhengzhou Metropolitan Circle (2018–2035)* 46; transport planning 45–46; *Zhengzhou Metropolitan Circle Transport Integrated Development Plan (2020–2035)* 46, 52
Zhoushan (Zhejiang province) 71, 73
Zhuhai (Guangdong province) 77, 80, 83

For Product Safety Concerns and Information please contact our EU
representative GPSR@taylorandfrancis.com
Taylor & Francis Verlag GmbH, Kaufingerstraße 24, 80331 München, Germany

www.ingramcontent.com/pod-product-compliance
Lightning Source LLC
Chambersburg PA
CBHW051758230426
43670CB00012B/2335